W9-CJO-973

1929

Christopher Hollis

June 1. 1969

DR. JOHNSON

Sam: Johnson.

DR. JOHNSON

BY

CHRISTOPHER HOLLIS

NEW YORK
HENRY HOLT AND COMPANY

First Edition

PRINTED IN THE
UNITED STATES OF AMERICA

This book is dedicated to

E. S. P. HAYNES

In the writing of it I have received suggestions and assistance of one sort or another from a large number of people. I should like especially to express my thanks to my mother, who was kind enough to read the proofs, and to Father Richard Mangan, S.J., Mr. E. S. P. Haynes, and Mr. Philip Bell.

C. H.

CONTENTS

ILLUSTRATIONS

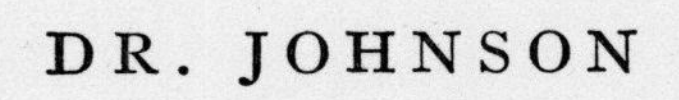

DR. JOHNSON

CHAPTER I

JOHNSON THE TORY

To sit down and write about Samuel Johnson may seem a very extraordinary thing to do. Assuredly no man of the world's history has been better written about than he, and I am far from flattering myself that any who have not had the curiosity to read about him in the pages of Boswell or Fanny Burney or Mrs. Piozzi, or in the commentaries on those pages which have been produced by a host of later writers, are very likely to have the curiosity to read about him here.

Johnson was one of the first, if not the first, of the recorded talkers of history. Almost alone of all the great figures of the past he survives for us, not for what he did, but for what he was. His triumph is the triumph of personality. Even in his own day, it is true, it was common to prefer his talk to his writing; while, if the modern world does not read Johnson, which is the fool—Johnson or the modern world? Have we managed our own affairs so wholly successfully as to entitle us to dictate to history upon what is right and wrong and what is good and bad? Yet Macaulay's paradox remains a truth, and a striking, if exaggerated, truth. "The reputation of those writings," he says of Johnson, "which he probably expected to be immortal is every day fading; while those peculiarities of manner and that careless table-talk, the memory of which he probably thought would die with him, are likely to be remembered as long as the English language is spoken in any quarter of the globe."

It is perhaps Johnson's posthumous fate to be punctually pronounced unreadable by people who have never tried to read him. Yet he is of the company that has made England, and you cannot neglect him without neglecting a part of England.

It is not rhetoric which writes thus. There is a certain amalgam of likes and dislikes, pleasures, prejudices and opinions which go to make up what is known as the English character. Of great writers some, such as Milton or Shelley, have criticised this character from the outside. Others, such as Chaucer or Dickens, have accepted it, and, as sharers in it, been content to give to it coherent expression. Of this latter class was Johnson. Wit, Pope has told us, is

> What oft was thought but ne'er so well expressed.

The ordinary man, as he reads Johnson, finds himself continually thanking Johnson for giving expression to what he himself had always thought. The ordinary man would have talked like Johnson, if he had been able to; not only could he not have written like Shelley, but he would not have written like him even if he could.

Samuel Johnson is to all wise men not a name but a friend. We, too, were at the Kings' Head in Ivy

Lane, Paternoster Row. We, too, have cried with Goldsmith, "with an air of superiority, like that of an esoteric over an exoteric disciple of a sage of antiquity, 'I go to Miss Williams.'" And the temptation is to talk of Johnson simply as one does talk of an old friend before another friend—to fold one's legs and have out the talk, as he would himself have said. It is thus that Johnsonians should talk to one another. Anecdote should be thrown back on anecdote and repartee on repartee. Yet to write thus is not, I suppose, defensible. Anecdote and repartee are, after all, in Boswell and he who loves them will wish to read them in Boswell. The world is too full of books for it to be excusable to make another by merely copying Boswell out.

If one would write about Johnson, it is necessary then to find something to say about him. It is not enough to tell the world that he was born at Lichfield, or that he gave oysters to his cat, or what he said about a woman preaching, for the world knows all these things already. It is necessary to try and find out what was the philosophy from which came the great company of repartees—how far it was a coherent philosophy and how far it was mere prejudice. It is necessary to explain how it was that a man who did not know the top from the bottom of a picture was the greatest friend of Joshua Reynolds, that a man without a note of music in his head was one of the greatest friends of Dr. Burney, that a man who loathed Whiggery was one of the greatest friends of

Edmund Burke, who loathed the stage was loved by David Garrick, who loathed Scotchmen was followed through life by the devotion of James Boswell, who thought patriotism "the last refuge of a scoundrel" was honoured by the admiration of Paoli, who—perhaps strangest of all—loved domestic virtue loved also Topham Beauclerk.

Mr. Gerald Gould, in a recent article, has suggested that Johnson is but the creation of us moderns, anxious, in our day of shifting values, to personify some great figure of the fixed standards. Everything that we admire in Toryism we have crowded on to Johnson, the Tory. One does not lightly disagree with so wise a man as Mr. Gould, and indeed there is a kernel of truth in his theory. In some things Goldsmith was a better Tory than Johnson; in some things Johnson was hardly a better Tory than Carlyle. We are apt to forget those things. Yet, even when we have remembered them, they are not sufficient to explain away Johnson. You cannot explain away Johnson unless you also explain away Reynolds and Burke and Paoli and Goldsmith and all the rest—great men who were yet willing simply to take Johnson's primacy for granted as hardly any other man has been taken for granted in all history. Least of all can you explain away Johnson by saying that Boswell was the great man. For it is obvious that the greater you make Boswell the greater do you make Johnson. A fool might have wasted his life in hero-worship of a bully, but greatness can only be repaid by greatness, as love can only be repaid by love.

Samuel Johnson was born at Lichfield in the year 1709. It is difficult to imagine him as a boy, and the reason for that difficulty is clear. He was over fifty before he met Boswell. All his friends of the club, all with whom he associated during his famous years, all who afterwards wrote about him, were people much younger than himself. Only of the old sage did they leave us living portraits. For the young Johnson they had, as we have, to draw upon their imagination.

Johnson's father was Michael Johnson, a bookseller of the cathedral city of Lichfield, a Tory. Of life in a cathedral city at the beginning of the eighteenth century Johnson has given us no very exact picture. Doubtless it was a dull affair. All that he cared to remember of it was "all the decent people at Lichfield getting drunk every night," and that "Forty years ago, sir, I was in love with an actress here, Mrs. Emmet, who acted Flora in *Hob in the Well.*"

From his father Johnson learnt those political principles which writers have been only too ready to waive away as prejudices, when they have found themselves unable to refute them by argument. And before we come, as we later shall come, to consider the especial Toryism of Johnson, it would be perhaps as well to state here what we understand to be the general meaning of the word "Tory."

The basis of Toryism is then the acceptance of

status. It is the belief of the Tory that people are happiest in a society which provides for each a settled station, to which he is born and which he accepts, obeying those above him so long as they exercise powers which are rightly theirs, but not thinking them his superiors; ordering those below him, but not thinking them his inferiors. As Johnson said in a wise phrase of impartial rebuke to snob and leveller, "Every man is to take existence on the terms on which it is given to him."

The belief of the Tory is that it is important *that* the question of a man's position in the world should be settled; but *how* it is settled, is less important. Making good very rarely makes people good. Success, which panders to desire, brings, not happiness, but disappointment.

Such a political belief is clearly very easily combined with a belief in supernatural religion. Not in the competitions of this world, but in the contemplation of timeless reality, can a rational being find satisfaction. As Sir Thomas Browne has said, that master of text-books for Tories:

> "Earthly inequalities . . . may be contentedly allowable in the affairs and ends of this world, and in suspension unto what will be in the order of things hereafter and the new system of mankind which will be in the world to come; when the last may be the first and the first the last; when Lazarus may sit above Cæsar and the just obscure on earth shall shine like the sun in Heaven; when

personations shall cease and histrionism of happiness be over; when reality shall rule and all shall be as they shall be for ever."

Where Toryism is not found in combination with definite religious belief, it is probably found in combination with pessimistic scepticism. With the vague worship of kindliness it mixes very ill.

One man must be subordinate to another if society is to survive. Toryism proclaims that the precedence of society is frankly arbitrary. The King is King simply because someone has to be and he happens to be; Michael Johnson finds himself a bookseller and remains a bookseller. There is, as Lord Melbourne said of the Garter, "no damned nonsense of merit about it." There is no pretence that a man has risen to the top of the tree by deserving to do so, nor that a career is open to talents.

Thus the last King of England, in Johnson's opinion, was Charles II. He was the last King who had had the power of accepting his position without either arrogance or that false humility which is a mere shirking of responsibility. Since Charles's death things had gone from bad to worse, until the improvement under George III, to whom Johnson was afterwards to pay what was, in his mouth, the tremendous compliment of saying that he was as great a gentleman as Charles II.

> Fallitur egregio quisquis sub principe credit
> Servitium.

Johnson lived before Macaulay. So large has been Macaulay's influence that even to-day, though one may correct him on details, to question his general version of English seventeenth-century history is to seem a wilful paradox-monger. Yet Johnson was conscious of no paradox. For good or for bad, his interpretation is different from that of the nineteenth-century Whig.

> "Charles the Second was licentious in his practice; but he always had a reverence for what was good. Charles the Second knew his people and rewarded merit. The Church was at no time better filled than in his reign. He was the best King we have had from his time till the reign of his present Majesty, except James the Second, who was a very good king, but unhappily believed that it was necessary for the salvation of his subjects that they should be Roman Catholics. He had the merit of endeavouring to do what he thought was for the salvation of the souls of his subjects till he lost a great empire. We, who thought that we should not be saved if we were Roman Catholics, had the merit of maintaining our religion at the expense of submitting ourselves to the government of King William, for it could not be done otherwise—to the government of one of the most worthless scoundrels that ever existed. No; Charles the Second was not such a man as —— [naming another king]. He did not destroy his father's will. He took money, indeed, from

France; but he did not betray those over whom he ruled: he did not let the French fleet pass ours. George the First knew nothing and desired to know nothing; did nothing and desired to do nothing; and the only good thing that is told of him is that he wished to restore the crown to its hereditary successor."

He roared with prodigious violence against George the Second.

It may be objected that the price of Tory philosophy is a less efficient state than that which could be procured by a more Napoleonic system. Whether that objection be true or false, and, if it is true, how important a truth it is, this is not the place to consider. One must be careful to avoid the danger of trying to make society impossibly rigid. Some avenue, such as that of the Church in the Middle Ages, must be provided by which the person who is quite unable to adapt himself to the state of life into which he is born may have an opportunity to escape from it. Of this sane Toryism was very well aware. The question is not whether people shall be allowed, but whether they shall be encouraged to better themselves, whether the normal man shall be encouraged to be contented or discontented. Johnson's opinion was that he should be encouraged to be contented. He would, for instance, have had the Lord Mayors of London succeed by seniority, even though he admitted that you would then have many very incompetent Lord Mayors, "for," he argued, "the evil of competition is greater than that of the worst mayor that can come." Politics in his day, he was to complain, "had come to be little more than the art of rising." That was the Johnsonian version of Napoleon's *"Carrière ouverte aux talents."*

Toryism, then, allows to politics only a small part in the making or marring of human happiness. The poor man, if he wishes to do so, can learn the love of beautiful things; he can kneel in a church; he can marry; he can beget children; he can collect his friends and go and drink with them in a tavern. By these things, and by such things as these, is happiness given rather than by the scrambles of man against man for fame or precedence or power. As Johnson wrote in Goldsmith's poem:

> How small of all that human hearts endure
> That part which kings or laws can cause or cure.

> "The duration of Parliament," he said, "whether for seven years or the life of the King, appears to me so immaterial that I would not give half a crown to turn the scale one way or the other. The Habeas Corpus is the single advantage which our Government has over that of other countries."

Liberalism gives a larger importance to political things. The difference between it and Toryism may perhaps be put thus: Liberalism guarantees the liberties of the extraordinary man, Toryism of the ordinary man. Thus Liberalism demands that everyone who wants to write a pamphlet should be allowed to write a pamphlet, Toryism that everyone who wants to have a drink should be allowed to have a drink. Of those liberties which the ordinary man does not wish to exercise it is more contemptuous—perhaps, in all but the sanest Toryism, too contemptuous. Be that as it may. Take, at any rate, Johnson's excellent sense about the liberty of the Press.

> "They make a rout about universal liberty without considering that all that is to be valued, or indeed can be enjoyed by individuals, is private liberty. Political liberty is good only so far as it produces private liberty. Now, sir, there is the liberty of the Press, which you know is a constant topic. Suppose you and I and two hundred more were constrained from printing our thoughts: what then? What proportion would that restraint upon us bear to the private happiness of the nation?"

Or his characteristic comment on the fuss of the Middlesex election.

> "A Government, of which an erroneous or an unjust representation of Middlesex is the greatest crime that interest can discover or malice can upbraid, is government approaching nearer to perfection than any that experience has known or history related."

It is then important to get some notion of the position in the world to which such a man as Michael Johnson would expect his son to aspire. He would expect him to grow up ready to accept the rule of a governing class to which he did not belong. He would equally expect him to grow up conscious of his dignity as a man even before members of that governing class, ready to behave, indeed, as his son did afterwards behave before Lord Chesterfield or the dons of Pembroke, as ready to write of a courtier as one "whose business is to watch the looks of a being weak and foolish as himself" as he was to knock down the insolent Osborne, the bookseller, or to toss from the circle into the stalls the rash man who stole his seat in the theatre. Indeed, one cannot better sum up Johnsonian Toryism than by saying that it is built upon the Socratic maxim of each man to his trade and the Christian dogma of the equality of man. "The scholar's rank, like the Christian's," Johnson was to say, "levels all distinctions of rank." "But in this," engagingly adds that gorgeous fool, Sir John Hawkins, "he was mistaken." The relationship of governor to governed Johnson expressed in the phrase "a casual superiority over those who are by nature equal to us."

One day, when the matter happened to crop up in conversation, Johnson said to Boswell, "You are a gentleman; I am not." Johnson certainly was not a gentleman—that is, he was not born into the governing class—nor would he ever have dreamed of claiming to be. He could hardly tell who was his grandfather. Yet he did not for that reason think that Boswell was in any way a better man than he.

Still less was the accident that Boswell had inherited certain social duties from which he himself was exempt any reason why they should not argue with one another across a tavern-table in perfect equality. About the governing class he had no more illusions than had his enemy, Lord Chesterfield, whom he so curiously resembled and from whom he so curiously differed. Their opinions upon it were very similar. "It is wonderful, sir," said Johnson, "with how little real superiority of mind men can make an eminent figure in public life." Such figures were, to quote Carlyle, but "as apples or horse-dung on the top of the current." Johnson never made the snob's blunder of confounding the lord with the man nor of imagining that the horse-dung propelled itself by its own energy.

When one runs through a list of his friends, one finds that they were chosen quite impartially from those who were and those who were not gentlemen. He had neither the snob's prejudice in favour of gentlemen nor the snob's prejudice against them. Boswell, certainly, was a gentleman; Garrick as certainly was not; Beauclerk and Langton were; Thrale, I suppose, not—Murphy says of him, with a certain carefulness of accuracy, that he had "the habits of a gentleman"—Goldsmith and Burke not—though the word has very little meaning when applied to an Irishman. Johnson, one may guess, would have understood very well the French revolutionary who objected to the concentration of political power into the hands of a class. He would have found it much harder to understand the modern attitude by which we all have a vote but one does not speak to the servants, by which we are free and equal and all privileges of rank are abolished, so we club together and elect a lord.

Everybody is familiar with the story of how Johnson challenged Mrs. Macaulay, the Radical, to prove the sincerity of her equalitarian opinions by bidding her butler sit down to her table. Not everybody remarks upon the most interesting lesson to be learnt from that story—the lesson that it does not, at that date, seem to have been thought especially odd to carry on such a conversation before a servant. The inequality between servant and master, from which we still suffer to-day, was, it seems, a special vice of Victorian England. The Continent has never properly had it. The Middle Ages did not have it. The Shakespearean masters and servants knew nothing of it, nor did the masters and servants of Sir Walter Scott. In the seventeenth century the Pepys sent for their servants to join in their games as a matter of course. Only the worst of the eighteenth century tried to insist on it.

It is characteristic that one of the first incidents in Johnson's life was that of being taken by his mother to be touched by Queen Anne. Johnson "had a confused but somehow a sort of solemn recollection of a lady in diamonds and a long black hood." As they returned from the touching in the stage-coach, he records, "We were troublesome to the passengers. . . . I was sick; one woman fondled me, the other was disgusted." One can believe it.

Macaulay jeers away the tale. Leslie Stephen is content to note that "disease and superstition stood by his cradle." It is, I think, foolish to dismiss it so cavalierly. Whether the Kings of England ever had a power of curing disease by a touch I do not know. The evidence is not conclusive. I am willing to be sceptical, but I am not willing to be more than sceptical. The King is a sacramental person. He has authority over his subjects because it has been conferred on him by God, and that God, while conferring the right to rule, should also have conferred the power to heal, does not seem to be inherently unreasonable. If the Johnsons were superstitious, they are to be blamed, for superstition is a great vice. Yet it seems that their conduct was rather that of the entirely rational sceptic. They thought that the evidence did not clearly show whether the touch was effective or not; to try it might do good and could not do harm. They tried, having no especial hopes, and, as is well known, it did no good.

All the world knows of the superficial oddities of Samuel Johnson—that he collected orange-peel; that he touched railings; that he contorted himself so queerly as sometimes to terrify those who saw him; that he rolled down a hill in Lincolnshire; that he ran a race with Baretti in the rain in Paris; that he ran another race with a young lady in Devonshire and kicked his shoes off that he might run the better; that he talked with Mrs. Thrale through a convent-grill; that he challenged a don, "eminent for learning and worth" and "of an ancient and respectable family in Berkshire," to climb a wall with him. All the world knows these things, and much of the world is content to know very little else about him, to think of him as a buffoon figure—as it were a Falstaff of reality, a subsidiary and historical member of the Pickwick Club. His oddities Johnson himself and Reynolds ascribed merely to habit. Doubtless they were caused, or partly caused, by some physical affliction, and, had he lived at a later date, science would have been able, if not to cure, at least to name them. In a ruder age such afflictions had to be suffered unchristened.

Yet Johnson, though he was, it must be admitted, extravagantly eccentric in the fields in which men ought to be moderately eccentric, yet was eccentric only in those fields. Men ought to think alike but behave differently, for reason is absolute, taste personal. Johnson certainly dressed differently from his contemporaries, if only because his linen was dirtier and his wig more scorched; where he thought differently from them, it was usually only because he thought better.

It is the fashion, on the other hand, to say that Johnson had a conventional mind. Strictly, it is not possible to have a conventional mind. It is possible to have conventional opinions, but reason a man either uses or he does not use. Conventional opinions I do not think that Johnson did have. Often, it is true, his opinion agreed with the conventional opinion, as does that of every sensible person. But it would be difficult—though, I admit, not impossible—to find a conventional opinion of his that was not also a true opinion. If that be so, you have proved nothing by your catalogue of his conventional and true opinions. For you have not proved whether he went for his opinions to convention or to reason. It is easier to test him where he was clearly at fault.

Johnson's largest deficiency was, I suppose, his lack of æsthetic feeling. For poetry, in the strict sense of the word, he cared little. His dictionary, for instance, defines it merely as "metrical composition." Pope's *Iliad* was to him "a performance which no age or nation can pretend to equal," and he asked, as if it were a rhetorical question, "If Pope be not a poet, where is poetry to be found?" He cared nothing for painting. "I have heard him say," writes Mrs. Thrale, "that he should sit very quietly in a room hung round with the works of the greatest masters and never feel the slightest disposition to turn them if their backs were outermost." He did not believe that there was such a thing as music except for the somewhat unconvincing reason that King David seems to have cared for it. Some French horns at a Freemason's funeral at Rochester made upon him "an impression of a melancholy kind." But this was "the first time I have ever been affected by musical sounds"—and, it seems, the last. "Music," he observed, "is less unpleasant than other noises." Hearing it said of a certain musical performance that it was very difficult, he replied, "I wish that it had been impossible." The learned and conscientious compiler of *A Million Facts* has told us that music "has a soothing effect on the hippopotamus." But Johnson, of whom it is recorded that he laughed like a rhinoceros, at least refused to be soothed like the hippopotamus.

This æsthetic incapacity it is important to remember when we come to talk of his general pessimism. The window of beauty, through which it is given to others to catch a glimpse of the substance that is behind our passing unreality, was a window through which he could never look. Absorbed in the contacts of a shouting, vivid, perishing world, he could never have begun to guess what Keats meant by saying that "a thing of beauty is a joy for ever."

Now these opinions, though as wrong as any opinions can be, are surely not stupid opinions. Certainly they are not conventional opinions. We must admit that Johnson was himself all but incapable of æsthetic appreciation. The merely conventional man would, under such an incapacity, adopt the conventional attitude—rave, lie, exclaim "How beautiful!" "How exquisite!" "How can people bear to live without art?" Every concert-hall and picture-gallery is full of such men and women. It is the last attitude which we can imagine Johnson adopting.

What then is there to be said for his Philistinism? Once you admit that he was himself deficient in æsthetic feelings, then you must admit that it was only possible for him to approach beauty as an external investigator. He had to observe such people as laid claim to this special æsthetic emotion and decide whether or not their claim was just. Now there is certainly no reason why there should not be an absolute beauty, just as there is no reason why there should not be genuine mystical experience. At the same time it is very hard to see *a priori* why there should be such things. Read the ninety-fourth *Rambler* and you will see what a good case Johnson can make for doubting the existence of beauty. Most of the people who claim to perceive are certainly liars, and it is a petulant, but a very natural, blunder to exclaim hastily that they are all liars. Certainly such a judgment is false; it is the judgment of an impatient man, but it is not the judgment of a fool. Least of all is it the judgment of a conventional man.

I have taken an instance where he was wrong. Let me take another where he was right.

A hostess one day receives from a guest, who has deserted her without warning, the following letter:

> "MADAM,—I beg your pardon for the abruptness of my departure in the morning, but I was compelled to it by conscience. Fifty years ago, Madam, on this day I committed a breach of filial piety. My father had been in the habit of attend-

ing Uttoxeter market and opening a stall there for the sale of his Books. Confined by indisposition, he desired me that day to go and attend the stall in his place. My pride prevented me; I gave my father a refusal. And now to-day I have been at Uttoxeter; I went into the market at the time of business, uncovered my head and stood with it bare for an hour on the spot where my father's stall used to stand. In contrition I stood and I hope that the penance was expiatory."

Any epithet in the dictionary would seem more suitable to such conduct than that of "conventional." A conventional man does not go and stand in the rain at Uttoxeter in order to atone for a piece of rudeness of which he had been guilty fifty years before. A rational man perhaps does. For although it is common to speak of penance and punishment as relics of barbarism, yet to do so is a foolishness of which Johnson was never guilty. He once told the abbess of a convent that she was there, "not for the love of virtue, but the fear of vice." And she answered that "she should remember this as long as she lived." "There are many good men," he said at another time, "whose fear of God predominates over their love." "The fear of the Lord" was, he knew well, not, indeed, the end of wisdom or the last word in it, but "the beginning of wisdom," and the human race is not such that very many penetrate beyond the beginning.

For this reason—because, if you like to put it in theological terms, of his profound belief in original sin—he had always a great dislike of government by the weapon of what he used to call "cant" but what modern language would call "idealism."

Women were to him a fact to be faced, and marriage a sacrament. He denounced, for instance, the Royal Marriage Act, which purported to give the King power to dissolve the marriages of princes entered into without his consent. Even the King, he said, could not undo a marriage. For marriage did not "depend upon the will of man." Marriage was a sacrament and might, as *Rasselas* and the *Rambler* show him to have known, very easily become a tragedy, "though even ill-assorted marriages are preferable to cheerless celibacy," and though his own affection for his wife was such that, unless the accounts of her which Garrick has given us are grossly libellous, it must be ascribed at least as much to the weakness of his eyesight as to the warmth of his heart. Yet he never fell under the sentimental illusion that the kingdom of the family could be governed without a king. Resolved "not to be made the slave of caprice," Johnson, as he and his wife rode to their wedding, deliberately pushed on ahead and out of her sight, in order to reduce her to tears and force her to recognise her dependence on him.

I do not say that this was a good thing to have done. Indeed it was bad and brutal, and there was a certain brutality in Johnson which made him say things which every man knows to be true about woman's attitude towards sex but which most men pretend that they have not discovered. Take, for instance:

> "I have always thought the clamours of women unreasonable who imagine themselves injured because the men who followed them upon the supposition of a greater fortune reject them when they are discovered to have less. I have never known any lady who did not think wealth a title to some stipulations in her favour: and surely what is claimed by the possession of money is justly forfeited by its loss."

It is even perhaps easy to represent as altogether brutal Johnson's whole attitude towards marriage. To do so would be, I think, unfair, and his love for his wife is a proof that it would be unfair. When he said that marriages would be as happy if they were all arranged by the Lord Chancellor, he meant, not that love was a thing to be laughed at, but that it was a thing to be created by mutual service and sacrifice —by a service and sacrifice that could only exist between married people. "The disproportions of absurdity grow less and less visible as we are reconciled by degrees to the deformity of a mistress." The regular union created in familiarity a relation less negative. The passion of love might be an indication of the possibility of love, but it was not itself love. His argument was not so much that marriage should be undertaken without love as that love was impossible without marriage. Love was the creation of marriage.

Passionately, for instance, though he was devoted to the memory of his wife, yet he said of another lady that, if he had married her, "I do not know but it might have been as well." Marriage did, as it happened, create the relationship of love between him and Tetty Johnson. It might have created it between him and another.

How far he was right we need not decide. At the least his opinion upon marriage was not that which the English think that the French hold when they speak of *un mariage de convenance*. He was not, it is true, a romantic. He protested, for instance, against Dryden's pandering to the immoral and false notion of "the romantick omnipotence of Love." The passion of love was to be resisted, where it was right to resist it, as much as was any other passion. Yet he did not believe that love was a thing that could be laid on like the hot and cold water and let into the bath at convenience.

From the same distrust of uncontrolled emotion sprang his opinions upon education. He would have had little sympathy with the spirit of Arnold and Sir Henry Newbolt, nor with the schoolmaster who appeals to the boy to do "for the sake of the school" some unpleasant thing which the master would otherwise have to do for himself. "I hate by-roads in education," he said.

A boy at school has to be made to do many things which he dislikes doing. There are three ways in which he can be compelled to do such things. An appeal can be made to his "school spirit," and this appeal, though perhaps successful, may only succeed at the expense of creating a spirit of unreasoning and patriotic priggishness which is more harmful than the violation of a hundred school rules. Much of English public school patriotism is sane and healthy. But in much of it also there is a kind of consecration of lying, which is so very offensive and so very dangerous. There is thought to be something vaguely un-English in even trying to tell the truth about, say, the general merits of one's school. Secondly, a competition can be organised and the performance of the task ensured by making it a matter of winning or losing. This again is harmful, for it encourages to compete. Thirdly, there is the old-fashioned theory that, where reason is not strong enough to see why a thing should be done, it is least harmful to enforce it by the mere fear of punishment. This theory Johnson held.

His own schoolmaster, Hunter, had never taught his pupils. Rather, Johnson explained, "he whipped and they learnt"—a division of labour for which Johnson does not seem to have thought much the worse of him.

"I would rather," he said, "have the rod to be the general terror of all to make them learn than to tell a child, if you do thus or thus, you will be more esteemed than your brothers or sisters. The rod produces an effect which terminates in itself. A child is afraid of being whipped and gets his task, and there's an end on't; whereas by exciting emulation and comparisons of superiority, you lay the foundation of lasting mischief."

It is but fair to add that Johnson was himself always markedly kind to children—one of the minor triumphs of his life was when he induced Dr. Sumner to abolish holiday-tasks—and a very unsuccessful schoolmaster.

In his hatred of "cant," doubtless, is to be found the answer to the much-debated question why Johnson never took Holy Orders. Into the controversy upon the exact shade of his Churchmanship it is not necessary to enter. Some would have it that he was all but a Catholic, and tell us that old Mr. Langton thought till his dying day that Johnson was a Catholic; others claim him as a sturdy Protestant, and point to his behaviour concerning the Piozzi marriage as proof. It may well be, as is sometimes said, that, if Johnson had been born in a Catholic country, he would have fitted very well into its society. It would be as valuable to say that, if he had not had such short sight, he would have seen better. We must speak of the actual Johnson that was, not of a hypothetical Johnson that might have been.

Now Johnson was much more interested in the

doctrines which Protestants and Catholics held in common than in those upon which they differed. Yet, since so much of Protestantism has to-day abandoned so many of those common doctrines, such a position makes him appear to us very much more Catholicly minded than he would ever have appeared to himself. Dean Inge has very legitimately told Protestants, and they have since been very legitimately telling one another, that their name is not negative but positive. Protestants do not "protest against"; they "strongly affirm." If that be so (as it is), then I suppose that the most distinctive strong affirmation of Protestantism is that of the appeal to the uninterpreted Bible. On such a test Johnson was most certainly a Protestant. Of a disputed doctrine or practice he always asked if it was scriptural, never if it was according to the mind of the Church. "Tradition, sir," he told Boswell, "has no place where the Scriptures are plain."

It is true that the *Journey to the Western Islands* is filled with much praise of "the Romish clergy" and the old religion, yet such praise was mainly, I think, merely a stick with which to beat the modern Presbyterians. Where it was more than that, it was but the admiration of a good man for goodness wherever he might happen to find it. Indeed, so far is the *Journey* from being a Catholic tract that Father Adams, the Jesuit philologist, dismisses it as the work of "that ungraceful and depreciating cynic, Dr.

Johnson." Johnson was no forerunner of an Oxford Movement.

It was doubtless his very Protestantism which kept him a layman. Had circumstances been different, he might very well have become a priest. He could never have become a preacher. He might easily have allowed himself to become the instrument of the sacraments. But, moralist though he was, he was a man of too much humour and too much sense to accept a titular moral leadership of his fellows. Morality was to him a thing too awful for the casual rant of a Sunday pulpit.

CHAPTER II

THE IMPORTANCE OF GRUB STREET

In 1728 Johnson went up to Pembroke College, Oxford. Dr. Adams would have it that his career there at least resembled that of the ordinary undergraduate. Johnson's own story was that he "passed a morning, in compliance with the customs of the place, at his tutor's chambers, but, finding him no scholar, went no more." At any rate, he came down without a degree, and of his life at Oxford we are left with little more than the tantalising half-confidences of a later day, to know more of which we would give many *Ramblers*. How grateful, for instance, should we be for details of the night when he took "three bottles of port without being the worse for it!" "University College hath witnessed this," is the challenging but the only commentary on the feat; "the rest is silence." Again, when the old man was nearly seventy, Boswell visited Pembroke in his company.

"We walked with Dr. Adams into the Master's garden and into the common-room. *Johnson* (after a reverie of meditation): Ay! Here I used to play at draughts with Phil. Jones and Fludyer.

Jones loved beer and did not get very forward in the Church."

Of Phil. Jones history has, I fancy, left us but one other record—the quaint entry in the Pembroke College buttery-book, across one page of which is scrawled:

"Oyes, oyes, come forth, Phil. Jones, and answer to your charge for exceeding the batells."

To have played draughts with Dr. Johnson, to have drunk, to have "exceeded the batells," to have failed—what a curious immortality!

The pious have picked out the course of Johnson's life between his leaving of the University in 1731 and his coming up to London in 1737. He was sometimes pedagogue, sometimes translator, and both professions he loathed. After six years he could bear no more, and with a tragedy in his pocket—of all unpromising letters of introduction—"one Johnson," to quote a letter of Gilbert Walmisley, set out for London in the company of a pupil of his named David Garrick, determined, as he said, "to drive the world about a little."

It is the fashion to say that at that date it was much more difficult to make money by the pen than it is at this. This fashion, since modern etiquette demands that people should not tell the truth about their incomes, it has not been possible to expose. Yet it is not so crudely true as is pretended. Doubtless there was more real distress among writers than there is to-day. The Grub Street tales that one can pick out of volumes of eighteenth-century reminiscences very amply prove that, and the reason of it is easy to see.

Though in the eighteenth century there was a tolerable market for the book-writer, yet the book-writer, if he was to live by his pen, had to live almost entirely by his books. Journalistic jobs were very few. No young man to-day, without either a name or a penny, would dream of setting up in London and expecting to make a living at once merely out of his books. It would be impossible to-day; it was as impossible in the eighteenth century. The only strange thing about the eighteenth century was that so many people should have attempted this impossibility. Grub Street, one feels, had, after all, only itself to thank. No one was compelled to live there, and most who chose to live there must have soon regretted their choice. Johnson must often, in his early days in London, have come to see the sound sense in the suggestion of one of the first booksellers to whom he applied—that "it would be his wisest course to buy a porter's knot and carry trunks."

At the one end of the scale, then, it must be admitted, there was the company of Grub Street, who, we are told, lived in a condition of destitution to which there is probably no parallel among journalists to-day, though I am myself more than half inclined to agree with Professor Saintsbury's scepticism about the reality of this society and though God knows that even to-day among the motley army of ghosts and free lances who haunt the slums of the newspaper world are to be found lives not so notably more affluent than those of Savage or of the dunces of the *Dunciad.*

At the other end of the scale, compulsory education, which has given to everyone in the country a certain capacity to read, has created a quite new class—the best-seller writer—who makes, if not by his pen, at the least by his dictaphone, sums many times greater than anybody ever made in the eighteenth century. Cheap printing has brought it about that scarcely any are so poor that they cannot afford to pay someone else to do their thinking for them. This privilege was previously confined to the more well-to-do.

Yet between these two classes came the men who, having acquired a certain position, wrote good books on sensible subjects. This third class—the class to which Johnson came to belong—seems, from the figures, to have done very fairly well for itself. Leslie Stephen has made an interesting collection of the fees which some of such men received.

"The copyright of Tillotson's sermons was sold, it is said, upon his death for £2,500. . . . It is said that 4,600 people subscribed to the two posthumous volumes of Conybeare's Sermons. . . . Young made more than £3,000 for the Satires, called the *Universal Passion,* published, I think, on the same plan; and the Duke of Wharton is said, though the report is doubtful, to have given him £2,000 for the same work. Gay made £1,000 by his poems, £400 for the copyright of the *Beggar's Opera,* and three times as much for its second part, *Polly.* Among historians, Hume seems to have received £700 a volume; Smollett made £2,000 by his catch-penny rival publication; Henry made £3,300 by his history; and Robertson, after the booksellers had made £6,000 by his *History of Scotland,* sold his *Charles V* for £4,500. Among the novelists, Fielding received £700 for *Tom Jones* and £1,000 for *Amelia;* Sterne for the second edition of the first part of *Tristram Shandy* and for two additional volumes received £650; besides Lord Faulconberg gave him a living (most inappropriate acknowledgment, one would say) and Warburton a purse of gold. Goldsmith received 60 guineas for the immortal *Vicar,* a fair price, according to Johnson, for a work by a then unknown author. By each of his plays he made about £500, and for the eight volumes of his *Natural History* received 800 guineas. Towards the end of the century Mrs. Radcliffe got £500 for the *Mysteries of Udolpho* and £800 for her last work, the *Italian.* Perhaps the largest sum given for a single book was £6,000 paid to Hawkesworth for his account of the South Sea Expedition. Horne Tooke received from £4,000 to £5,000 for the *Diversions of Purley;* and it is added by his biographer, though it seems to be incredible, that Hayley received no less than £11,000 for the *Life of Cowper.*"

If, then, one makes allowances for the altered value of money, it would seem that, though the little reporter on the provincial newspaper on the one hand and Nat Gould or Ruby M. Ayres on the other did well to be born when they were born, yet such writers as Dean Inge or Mr. Beerbohm would have been allowed to write a little better sense, and have been paid a little more money for writing it, had they been contemporaries of Dr. Johnson.

That it was possible to find writing men in the eighteenth century who did not possess all the money that they would have liked to possess I am very willing to believe. The phenomenon is peculiar neither to writing men nor to the eighteenth century. Johnson's own conclusion was to doubt whether "authors, however querulous, are in reality more miserable than their fellow-mortals." And the truth is surely that all men are equally unhappy, but that journalists—poor devils—have to make their bread and butter by saying so.

There could be no better proof that, with all its disadvantages, the living to be made out of literature compared favourably with that to be made out of other things than the fact that Johnson chose to live by it. No man could have had less respect, on the one hand, for the mere cant of the empty head which, unable to distinguish itself otherwise, pretends to suffer from a passion for self-expression, nor, on the other, less understanding of that very rare being, the true artist, to whom the world was well lost for beauty's sake. He hated the "foppery"—of which Congreve, for instance, was always guilty—of pretending to be a man of fashion who had written something by accident, and quoted with approval Voltaire's remark on this affectation in the *Lettres sur les Anglais*—"that, if he had been only a gentleman, he should not have come to visit him." "No man but a blockhead," Johnson said, "ever wrote except for money." If that be so, there must have been some amenity in the literary life if one who was certainly not a blockhead preferred to make his money by writing rather than in any other way. And a man who, in his worst years of destitution and at a time when he himself admitted that it was possible to live on £30 a year, received, as Johnson did, almost £50 for a translation of Father Paul Sarpi, which he never made, and yet was allowed to keep the money, has not too large a complaint against the generosity of the world. This Johnson would have been the first to admit.

Yet at the same time it would be a petty falseness to try and laugh away the insecurity and the horrors of the Grub Street life of the eighteenth century for an author who had not yet established himself. The tale of Boyse, for instance, is more vivid than pleasant. Boyse, since he could not afford to get up, stayed in bed, covered with a blanket with two holes in it through which his arms could pass, so that he might continue to write. According to Cibber's *Life*, when "his distresses so pressed as to induce him to dispose of his shirt," he used to "cut some white paper in strips, which he tied round his wrists and in the same manner supplied his neck. In this plight he frequently appeared abroad, with the additional inconvenience of want of breeches." Pathos almost destroys humour in such a story, as it does in that which is told by a begging letter from him that is to be found among the Sloane MSS.

> "You were pleased," he writes to Sir Hans Sloane, "to give my wife the enclosed shilling last night. I doubt not but that you thought it a good one, but, as it happened otherwise, you will forgive the trouble occasioned by the mistake."

The *Life of Savage*, also, is certainly one which it is more amusing to read than to have lived. Assuredly never was there a man who had a more hearty contempt for unnecessary whining than had Johnson, and yet to him the memory of those first years in London was so dreadful that he could hardly bear to recall it. All those evils which Virgil imagined to reside in the very mouth of hell Johnson thought to be "the concomitant of a printer's house."

Vestibulum ante ipsum, primisque in faucibus orci,
Luctus et ultrices posuere cubilia Curæ;
Pallentesque habitant Morbi, tristisque Senectus,
Et Metus et malesuada Fames, et turpis Egestas,
Terribiles visu formæ; Lethumque laborque.[1]

During these years he was but a Party hack, when he was lucky enough to be able to be that, and "a scribbler for a Party" he was afterwards to class in the company of "a Commissioner of Excise" as the two lowest of human beings. His unhappiness was soon to become so intense that he began to look upon his previous misery as a sort of content.

Johnson's manner was doubtless not one wholly favourable to a young man anxious for his first step. He was for a time, Murphy records, employed by Osborne, the bookseller, to make a catalogue of his stock. Not content merely to copy down the titles, Johnson used sometimes to look inside at the contents. To Osborne the reading of a book was a profitless waste of the time that should have been devoted to selling it. One day a dispute arose between them, and Johnson, as Murphy says, "seized a folio and knocked down the bookseller." Boswell used to deny the story, but, when he appealed to Johnson for support of his denial, Johnson's emendation showed that it was a detail rather than his spirit which had been

[1] Just in the gate and in the jaws of hell
Revengeful cares and sullen sorrows dwell,
And pale diseases and repining age,
Want, fear, and famine's unresisting rage;
Here toils and Death, and Death's half-sister Sleep,
Forms terrible to view, their sentry keep.
—DRYDEN.

View of Lichfield

misrepresented. "Sir," said he, "he was impertinent to me and I beat him; but it was not in his shop; it was in my own chamber."

Johnson's other employer was Cave, a better man than Osborne; indeed, a man of many virtues, able to see that in Johnson he had something more than another Grub Street hack, yet not of a mind ample enough truly to appreciate Johnson's genius nor his gusto. Cave was a man of humble birth, the son of a cobbler of Rugby. Born in the days before the public schools had become altogether a monopoly of the rich, he went to Rugby School, but was expelled thence for robbing the hen-roosts of the head-master's wife. Drifting up to London, he became, after a variety of adventures, the editor of the *Gentleman's Magazine*. Adventure did not bring with it geniality. "Cave had no great relish for mirth, but he could bear it," is the very tepid praise which Sir John Hawkins finds it possible to give to him.

Besides Cave and Johnson, there was on the staff of the *Gentleman's Magazine* a certain Guthrie, a pleasing character. He it was who wrote *A General History of the World, from the Creation to the Present Time*, making it up as he went along, and afterwards reviewed the book himself in the *Critical Review*, praising it highly.

It may be perhaps of interest to give the contents of a typical number of the magazine—the number which contained an article by Johnson on Father Paul Sarpi, intended as a puff for the translation of Sarpi's

History of the Council of Trent, which Johnson was never energetic enough to complete. The other features are the Parliamentary Debates—not, as yet, written by Johnson; "Observations on Lapland," by Guthrie; Dr. Booerhave's "Receipt for an Ulcer in the Bowels"; an article called "What is Love?"; a few inches of verse called "A Modest Epitaph"; a foot or eighteen inches on "Whether Conjugal Happiness Decreasing after Marriage is not a Discouragement to Matrimony"; rather less on "French Fashions Explored." It all sounds very like last Sunday's paper.

Johnson began to long again, it seems, for even the miseries of an usher's life—miseries which had, in the days when he enjoyed them, driven him in despair to Grub Street. And, after the publication of his poem, "London," he was grateful for the offices of Pope, who offered to use his influence with Swift to get him a Dublin degree, possessed of which he might, he thought, aspire to the "giddy ambition of an assistant-mastership with an income of £60 a year." He would rather "die upon the road to Dublin" than "be starved to death by translating for booksellers."

As has already been said, all those to whom we owe our knowledge of Johnson were people much younger than was he himself, and, with the single exception of Garrick, people whom he did not come to know until very much later in his life. From Garrick he seems in those years to have drifted apart, and of his experiences during them he was never afterwards willing to talk. We therefore know very little of what did happen to him. Yet we know a good deal of the common life of Grub Street, and those who do not know cannot learn better than by reading Johnson's own *Life of Savage.*

Savage was one of Johnson's strange companions in misery, and, if he was not the strangest of those companions, then it is certain that the lost chapters in Johnson's life would have made far more memorable reading than the chapters which have survived. Broadly, Savage was a man of many misfortunes, but, when every tribute has been paid to Johnson's charity, of no virtues at all—except, possibly, loquacity. In character Johnson was as unlike to Savage as any two men can ever have been to one another. In misadventure their lives may not have been dissimilar.

Savage claimed that he was the illegitimate son of Lord Rivers by Lady Macclesfield, and that he had been treated by his mother ever since his birth with an unnatural and an almost incredible brutality. She repudiated him; she gave him to a poor woman to bring up; she told his father that he was dead—thus preventing him from leaving his son a legacy—until Lord Rivers, utterly wearied of the insoluble problem of discovering exactly whom he had and whom he had not begotten, gave it up in despair, and left all his fortune instead "to about twenty paltry whores" —to quote the quaint, if vigorous, phraseology of Dean Swift. Lady Macclesfield, meanwhile, was trying her best to get her son hanged for murder.

This amazing story Savage had persuaded Johnson to believe. The rights and wrongs of it are to-day very difficult to come by. Lady Macclesfield herself, not unnaturally perhaps, always denied its truth, while it must be admitted that two strong points in Savage's favour are his recognition by Lord Tyrconnel, his putative mother's nephew, and by one of her acknowledged daughters. Aaron Hill, the eccentric poet, believed in him, and gave publicity to his grievances in the *Plaindealer*. Nevertheless, every definite statement which he made has been found, where it has been possible to test it, wholly false, and it is very difficult not to conclude that Johnson, a young man, was the victim of a vulgar impostor.

Yet Johnson, if deceived by Savage's claims, was at least not at all deceived by his character. He knew Savage for an utter blackguard. Yet even in such a man that great charity found more to love than to hate. Johnson never suggested that he deserved any praise for sticking to his friend. Rather did it clearly never occur to him to do anything else. A French critic, according to Sir Walter Raleigh, writes that the *Life of Savage* is a lesson on the danger of having to do with men utterly lacking in moral principle. Its lesson is, rather, that there are some who will not desert such men even in spite of that danger.

It is important then, if we are to judge Johnson's character, to have in mind some picture of what this existence of Grub Street was, whether that picture be derived from the *Life of Savage* or elsewhere. The experiences of such a life must have been wholly unpleasant; they were not by any means wholly bad for the character which could survive them at all. Johnson emerged from his real contact with misery with a hearty and attractive hatred of all society's canting and whining over sham and small and sentimental manufactured misery. He came from it, too, as one who had been to school in the college of life, and the lesson that he had learnt there had been that it is necessary to pass on many men judgments very different from those which are passed by the world, that has merely met them over a dinner-table.

On the one hand, he had learnt the grand lesson that there is a charity which "covereth a multitude of sins." "Harry Hervey," he said of a bad man who had helped him during those dark years, "was a vicious man, but very kind to me. If you call a dog Hervey, I shall love him." On the other hand, he had learnt not to condemn utterly any man, who, however ridiculous and inconsistent his belief, however ridiculously and inconsistently expressed in practice, had yet kept in his soul a little, struggling sense of the omnipotence of God, of the insubstantiality of the world, of the impotence of man. "Campbell," he said of a Scotch friend who possessed a considerable literary reputation in his own day but is perhaps chiefly interesting to posterity for his claim to have drunk thirteen bottles of port at a sitting—a claim which

Johnson did not disbelieve, provided only that he let "one glass evaporate" before he took another—"Campbell is a good man, a pious man. I am afraid he has not been in the inside of a church for many years; but he never passes a church without pulling off his hat. This shows he has good principles."

Macaulay was able to find in this story nothing better than the matter for a jeer against Johnson's superstition. But I think that it will be agreed that Macaulay jeering at Johnson's superstition cuts a very silly figure. His self-satisfied comment on Johnson's dictum is one of the most extraordinary that was ever written. "Spain and Sicily," he says, "must surely contain many pious robbers and well-principled assassins."

One can but gravely agree with the platitude. As he himself might have said, "Every schoolboy knows" that Spain and Sicily do contain many pious robbers and well-principled assassins. What of it? Johnson did not say that Campbell's practice was good, but that his principles were good—that is, his recognition that there was a God who made him, and that, when he passed the house of God, it was good that he should pay some outward token of respect. Johnson would have been the first to agree that it would have been better if Campbell had put his principles more fully into practice by a more proper performance of his religious obligations. That did not alter his good principles. So, too, with the robbers of Sicily. Doubtless it would be admirable if they could be persuaded to cease robbing and doubtless a belief in God ought to carry with it a belief in the wickedness of robbery. But it is hard to see how they would better themselves by merely remaining robbers and becoming atheists. I even doubt if they would be as much better off as Macaulay imagined if they ceased to be robbers but became Whigs—which is, I suppose, what he meant by having good principles.

When a man argues, in favour of "the principle of subordination," that a society in which each person has and accepts his certain place is the happiest society, it is very easy and very common, and doubtless often very just, to reply with an *argumentum ad hominem,* to point out that your opponent is, if not of the highest rank, at any rate one who comes comfortably high in the social scale, and that therefore it is very easy for him to approve of such an organisation. Against Johnson, at any rate, such a gibe can never be made. And those who hold to that giant and perishing thing, the Tory creed, can at least take strength from the thought that the great soul of Samuel Johnson, though it suffered every bitterness of misery, yet came out from its suffering unshaken in its conviction of the folly of discontent.

Yet he did not come out indifferent to the sufferings of the poor. Such indifference his Toryism never admitted. "A decent provision for the poor," he said, "is the true test of civilisation." He was rather a Tory because he believed, rightly or wrongly, that a Tory society, being the sort of society which most nearly corresponded to the needs of human nature, was that which gave the greatest happiness to the poor.

It was his opinion, founded perhaps on a combination of strong philosophy and constitutional melancholy, that human life was a sad affair.

> "It has been observed in all ages," he writes in his *Life of Savage,* "that the advantages of nature or of fortune have contributed very little to the promotion of happiness and that those whom the splendour of their rank or the extent of their capacity have placed upon the summits of human life, have not often given any just occasion to envy in those who look up to them from a lower station; whether it be that apparent superiority incites great designs and great designs are naturally liable to fatal miscarriages; or that the general lot of mankind is misery and the misfortunes of those whose eminence drew upon them an universal attention, have been more carefully recorded because they were more generally observed and have in reality been only more conspicuous than those of others, not more frequent or more severe."

The latter was certainly Johnson's real opinion. It was not that man was wicked; he was rarely very wicked. "He thought there was very little gross wickedness in the world, and still less of extraordinary virtue." "I hope," he said again, "that I have not lost my sensibility of good, but I hope likewise that I have lived long enough in the world to prevent me from expecting to find any action of which both the original motive and all the parts were good." It was his interesting experience that he had found men "worse in commercial dealings, more disposed to cheat than I had any notion of; but more disposed to do one another a service than I had conceived." He added, "And really it is wonderful, considering how much attention is necessary for men to take care of themselves and ward off immediate evils, it is wonderful how much they do for others."

The cause of human unhappiness lay rather in the very nature of pleasure, which was but the temporary satisfaction of a desire which man has ever with him. The lot of mankind was one of much sorrow. The life of the rich, the life of the poor, life in the town, life in the country—all were alike subject to this inevitable decree. The sight of Ranelagh affected him with the same feelings with which the sight of the Persian host affected Xerxes. He could "scarcely help wishing while one fondles a baby that it may never live to become a man, for it is so probable that when he becomes a man he should be sure to end in a scoundrel." The pleasures of society, he argued with Boswell, were no more than "struggles for happiness."

It maddened him to hear of anyone claiming to be perfectly contented. Sometimes he was outrageous in his resentment of such a claim. Somebody once maintained that his sister-in-law—who was present—was perfectly contented. "If your sister-in-law is really the contented being she professes herself, sir," said Johnson, "her life gives the lie to every research of humanity; for she is happy without health, without beauty, without money, and without understanding."

If the story be accurate—its source is not above suspicion—this was certainly brutal and utterly indefensible. Yet, even to condemn, it is necessary to understand what it is that is asking to be defended. Johnson had none of that real hatred of happy men which subconsciously dominates so much that passes under the name of social reform. His hatred was for lies. He would not believe that a person could be perfectly contented with what could not of its nature give perfect contentment.

The whole truth must be good, but partial truth is often so very brutal, and so few can see more than a very small part of truth, that it is a large question how right it is to smash up that system of lies by which we try to comfort ourselves. You are tempted to ask whether, if all that Johnson has to teach is that this life is a wretched affair, it is necessary to go back to the eighteenth century to learn such a lesson. The philosophy which can only tell desperate men that they ought to despair, or the shipwrecked sailor, clinging to the last plank, that he will soon be drowned, is neither a very useful nor a very noble one.

The answer to that, the case for brutality, is, I think, that in Johnson's brutality there is a kind of twisted comfort. His was not a complaint of universal vanity. "Whatever enlarges hope will exalt courage"—provided, naturally, that the hope is at all founded. What he did was to warn people that down certain roads—the roads of political reform, of commercial prosperity, of religious revolt, of the mere æsthete's boredom—very little happiness was to be found. We have neglected his advice, have laughed at him, have thought that the problem of human life was very easy when he told us that it was very difficult. To-day we are beginning to suspect that we were wrong and he was right. We set out with too large hopes, and, now that the hopes are blasted, the danger is that we will turn to a too large despair. Johnson was, at his worst, a savage bully in the violence with which he tore away the little, baseless fabrics of human comfort. But, if he destroyed a foolish hope, it was only that he might prevent an unnecessary despair. Has ever a wiser bit of general advice been given than the advice that "many of the blessings universally desired are frequently wanted because most men, when they should labour, content themselves to complain"?

To a very strong mind there is always the temptation to use its strength merely to destroy all the hopes and all the loves of weaker men and women; to surrender itself to the devil's scorn, as the mind of Swift surrendered itself when he wrote upon the envelope containing Stella's lock of hair, "Only a woman's hair." This is, I suppose, the worst of all temptations, and only the very greatest of the greatest wholly resist it. Dante was quite above it; Shakespeare by no means so. Johnson, in his worst moods of melancholy, never fell, but he was certainly tempted. And, when the complaint is made of him, as it is justly made, that he was unfair to Swift, the reason must be remembered. Swift had succumbed to this temptation of scorn—a temptation which Johnson had felt, had recognised for the one wholly evil thing outside hell and had hardly conquered.

All mankind were alike subject to the inevitable decree. Such was afterwards to become Johnson's opinion. Yet in these years he was not yet wholly free from what, in his later life, he would, rightly or wrongly, have classed as "cant." His first considerable work—a poem entitled *London,* in imitation of the Third Satire of Juvenal—appeared in May 1738. Its theme—a theme upon which it has been the familiar custom of sentimentalists of every generation to harp—was that of the contrast between the miseries of the town and the joys and sweet simplicity of country life. It is a theme as old at least as Horace, and, I do not doubt, a great deal older, and one which, of all themes, Johnson was later to come most heartily to dislike. "No, sir," he was to say, "when a man is tired of London he is tired of life, for there is in London all that life can afford."

Because he soon revolted against a merely Rousseauan insincerity and refused any longer to dupe himself with silly tales of milkmaids and nightingales and blackberries, the world is greatly the gainer. Yet it is impossible not to feel that in his later praise of London he had done little but react from cant to countercant. His *Thoughts on Agriculture* shows him to have been very well aware of the instability of a commercial, the stability of an agricultural, prosperity. "Depend upon it," he said one day during his Hebridean tour, in a prophecy that is proving itself only too sadly wise, "this rage of trade will destroy itself. You and I shall not see it; but the time will come when there will be an end of it." "Then," he added, "the proprietors of land only will be the great men." And it would have been well if in his refuge from Rousseau he could have found a resting-place with Goldsmith and his *Traveller*.

Every sane man would wish to spend some of his time in a capital. But if a man wishes to spend all his time there, his mind must be cramped. There is in London much that life affords, but there is not all that life affords. The full tide of human existence Johnson found at Charing Cross. Another great man —a very different sort of man from Johnson—also gave to Charing Cross an especial place in his life. To him shone all the traffic of Jacob's ladder which was pitched between it and heaven. Samuel Johnson and Francis Thompson shared their love of God and their love of Charing Cross; they shared, I daresay, little else. Yet both had, in their different ways,

by the vision splendid
Been on their way attended.

There is something very noble in the gusto with which Johnson, though without the smallest illusion concerning the sadness and the horrors of life, yet asked of it nothing but that it should be given to him more abundantly. In his company life was worth living, if only to hear the vigour and vitality with which he denied that it was worth living. He enjoyed misery more than most men enjoy happiness. Yet it would be foolish not to admit that he paid a certain price for this gusto. Throughout all his life, though enormously immersed in the "struggles for happiness" of his fellow-creatures, he never for a moment forgot that there was "a Kingdom that is not of this world," that he was a citizen of another country. For all that, he was not a mystic. He did not walk in the company of God. He did not feel the presence of God; he deduced it. And his logic had taught him the fear of God, which is "the beginning of wisdom," rather than the love of God, which is its reward and consummation. He was blind to much which a St. Teresa or a St. Francis knew, even to much which a Francis Thompson knew, and, had he at least recognised his deficiency, he would have been both a wiser and a better man. Let him who is as good a man as Samuel Johnson most fitly blame Samuel Johnson for not being as good a man as Francis of Assisi.

Johnson liked London because it provided him with conversationalists, and he took it as an axiom that you could get better conversation in London than elsewhere. By life in London he did not mean that uneasy drift from luncheon to luncheon and from tittle-tattle to tittle-tattle which is the life in London of the rich. Still less did he mean a mouth and ears glued to a telephone and a mind bounded by financial statistics. Nor did the eighteenth century provide that vague, vast field of half-activity in which the successful can to-day so easily lose themselves. Johnson never in his life addressed a meeting; he never acted in a charity tableau; he never read a paper to a society; he never joined a League for the Prevention of anybody doing anything. To know London was to "explore Wapping," to talk to prostitutes and carry them home on one's back, to preside at taverns, to practise with all the fullness with which it can possibly be practised Pope's teaching upon "the proper study of mankind." And, if one uses London thus, it is doubtless true that on an average it is possible to get better conversation there than elsewhere. Yet, even so, one can get plenty of good conversation in London, but one gets little very good conversation there.

London is "at the centre of things." And "things," to tell the truth, are sometimes overrated. In London one meets everywhere people who can tell you the name of the man who did this and can quote sentences from the last work of the man who wrote that. But London panders to the superficial. Talk in London is always about what people are doing. It is gossip, and it is rare to find there anyone who, ignorant perhaps of the latest names and the latest *mots* and the latest plays, has yet kept over his mind that strict discipline which does not allow him to say that a thing is proved when it is not proved and which is the one sane mark of an educated man. Such a man one must search out in some queer corner of the country. As Johnson himself said, "A man cannot know modes of life as well in Minorca as in London; but he may study mathematics as well in Minorca." Human nature being what it is, succumbing, as it so easily does, before distraction, he may study them better.

In the country time matters very much less than it does in London. This is the especial superiority of a country life. For a man who is forced to live too intolerably in time is forced to follow after pleasures instead of after happiness, since pleasures are momentary and in time. Happiness comes, not from a sensation, but from a state of mind; it is rational; it therefore makes appeal to that part of a man which is outside time. The pursuit of pleasure, as Johnson used often to say, is the largest cause of human unhappiness. For pleasure of its very nature crumbles away at the moment of attainment, leaving behind only desire. Life, it has been said, would be a happy enough affair if it were not for its pleasures.

In the hard school of Grub Street Johnson had learnt very well the lesson of misery.

> This mournful truth is everywhere confessed:
> Slow rises worth by poverty depressed,

he wrote. And again:

> All crimes are safe but hated poverty.
> This, only this, the savage law pursues;
> This, only this, provokes the snarling Muse.

Nor did he ever fall into the literary trick of pretending that a silly peroration was a substitute for a dinner. The more real is the distress, the more hateful is rant about it.

> And here a female atheist talks you dead—

incomparably the most vivid line of the poem—of how many modern movements and meetings and committees might it be aptly quoted!

Yet Johnson, even when he speaks on a theme so real to him as that of the miseries of poverty, is not quite able to keep himself free from a cant of which he was afterwards to become thoroughly ashamed.

> Of all the griefs that harass the distressed,
> Sure the most bitter is the scornful jest,

he wrote.

Such a complaint would have been, to the later Johnson, "a foppish lamentation." He was to loathe like poison the man or woman whose life was a continual blather of soul-storms. His constant prayer was to be relieved from "unprofitable sorrow." He "hated to hear people whine about metaphysical distresses when there was so much want and hunger in the world"; and, of all kinds of nonsense, "grand nonsense" was the worst. "Grand nonsense," he said, "is insupportable." The sentimentalists, he always argued with much truth, "pay you by feeling" —that is, they use up so much energy in feeling that they have none left for helping. "Pooh, madam," he was to ask Mrs. Carter, "who is the worse for being talked of uncharitably?" Uncharitable talk, it is a sad but certain truth, more often than not gives more pleasure to its hearers than it does harm to its victims.

If one turns from content to form, it is impossible, while admiring the vigour of phrase in Johnson's poem, not at the same time to notice how far the epigrammatist was from being a poet. The Marquess Wellesley, no mean judge, said, after long consideration concerning Johnson's Latin verses, that they were all very bad but that some of them might have been worse. His English verse was better than that. Indeed, there is nothing technically wrong in it; but at the same time there is nothing poetical. It gives to us no hint at all of any world wherein we do not ordinarily walk. Certainly he was not a great poet; I do not think that he was even a great versifier. Pope was not a poet as Keats or Shakespeare were poets. Yet verse under his hand served a very respectable purpose. Just as a river runs more strongly if it is dammed up between certain banks, so Pope's arguments hit more strongly because they are compressed into the very rigid limits of a very regular metre. The argument in Johnson's verse, on the other hand, is often very powerful, but I do not think that it ever owes its power to the verse. Rather does the argument manage with difficulty to carry the verse on its shoulders. We are glad to be told about the world by a man who knows it so well as Johnson does, and, because he knows the world so well, we are willing to pardon much, even to pardon verse. We are willing to pardon him when, wishing to tell us to look at the world, he tells us to

> Let observation with extensive view
> Survey mankind from China to Peru.

But where the argument flags the verse becomes frankly ludicrous. Let us take examples. At Greenwich Johnson describes himself as

> Struck with the seat that gave Eliza birth.

It is not a convincing line; while

> Forgive my transports on a theme like this.
> I cannot bear a French metropolis,

reminds one irresistibly of the more successful comic verse of Mr. Hilaire Belloc.

Yet *London,* whatever its deficiencies, at least won Johnson a name. It was soon followed by *Marmor Norfolciense,* the fiction of which was that an old inscription "in monkish rhyme," inveighing against Sir Robert Walpole, had been found in Norfolk. The two works attracted the attention of Pope. He declared that their author must be *deterré,* and wrote to Richardson concerning him.

"This is imitated by one Johnson who put in for a Public-school in Shropshire, but was disappointed. He has an infirmity of the convulsive Kind, that attacks him sometimes, so as to make Him a sad Spectacle. Mr. P. from the Merit of This Work which was all the knowledge he had of Him endeavour'd to serve Him without his own application, & wrote to my L[d]. gore, but he did not succeed. Mr. Johnson published afterwards another Poem in Latin with Notes the whole very Humerous call'd the Norfolk Prophecy.

"P."

During the early years of the 1740's Johnson had accepted from Cave the task of reporting the Parliamentary Debates for the *Gentleman's Magazine*. There was not at that date any regular reporters' gallery nor were reports permitted. All that Johnson could do was to glean from Cave and others the names of the speakers, the side on which they had spoken, and the gist of their arguments, and then himself compose appropriate speeches. The secret of the authorship did not come out until, some years afterwards at Foote's house, Francis, the father of Hastings's enemy, happened to praise a certain speech of Pitt, as he then still was, saying that it was "the best he had ever read." "There was nothing in Demosthenes," he added, "to equal it."

A conversation sprang up about the speech, during which Johnson remained silent, until at last he interrupted.

"That speech," he said, "I wrote in a garret in Exeter Street."

Francis asked how that could be.

"Sir," said Johnson, "I wrote it in Exeter Street. I never had been in the gallery of the House of Commons but once. Cave had interest with the door-keepers. He and the persons employed under him gained admittance; they brought away the subject of discussion, the names of the speakers, the side they took, and the order in which they rose, together with notes of the arguments advanced in the course of the debate. The whole was afterwards communicated to me, and I composed the speeches in the form which they now have in the Parliamentary Debates."

The company praised the impartiality of the reports.

"That is not quite true," said Johnson. "I saved appearances tolerably well, but I took care that the Whig dogs should not have the best of it."

Having discovered that they really had deceived, Johnson had afterwards great remorse for having written these reports. Certainly they are excellent reading wherever the subject is one that can at all retain our interest at this distance of time. Doubtless Hawkins's criticism of them is just. He complains that "the language of them is too good and the style such as none of the persons to whom the speeches are assigned were able to discourse in." The "Whig dogs" were neither the first nor the last of politicians to owe to a reporter's kindness the untangling of their metaphors and the completion of their sentences.

At a later date Johnson returned again to a theme similar to that of *London.* He wrote, in imitation this time of the Tenth Satire of Juvenal, *The Vanity of Human Wishes.* Juvenal's Tenth Satire is hardly a satire at all in the fierce sense which the word may bear when applied to the Third. Old age had brought serenity. Between Johnson's two works there was a similar contrast, even if there had not been a similar passage of time. His mind is still afflicted with his old problem of the necessary insufficiency of pleasure. But no longer is he content to put himself off with the glib assumption that human nature ceases to be human nature at the boundary of the City of London. Neither in town nor in country, he now sees, is it possible for pleasure to lead to happiness. It is the nature of appetite, if it be uncontrolled by reason, always to outrun satisfaction; and, to illustrate this, Johnson selects from history appropriate examples of the Vanity of Human Wishes. The solution to the problem, he has now learnt, is to be found, not in an imaginary rural Utopia, but in the reason. A thing tasted is a thing whose taste has the next moment perished; a thing known is a thing known for ever—"a joy," as Keats would have said, "for ever." Therefore Grub Street and the Tories have brought Johnson back to the old Aristotelian conclusion. True happiness is to be found only in the knowledge and contemplation of reality—or, if you prefer, in the love of God (there can be no difference, since God alone is reality).

> A healthful mind,
> Obedient passions, and a will resigned,

are the goods for which we should pray.

> With these celestial Wisdom calms the mind,
> And makes the happiness she does not find.

CHAPTER III

THE "RAMBLER," CHESTERFIELD, SHAKESPEARE, AND VOLTAIRE

In the same year in which he wrote *The Vanity of Human Wishes* appeared also Johnson's tragedy, *Irene*. It is a fantastic performance, a tale of Greek and Turkish war. Blank verse to Johnson was merely appropriately chopped-up prose. To his unmusical ear it meant nothing. He attempted it only out of a puzzled desire to conform to an unintelligible convention. It must be some of the worst that the world has ever seen. Of it the less said the better. Yet of *Irene* one might write, as Johnson himself wrote of Prior's *Carmen Seculare*, "I cannot but suspect that I might praise or censure it by caprice without danger of detection; for who can be supposed to have laboured through it?" Yet I have laboured through it, nor is there any more to be said of it than that it is as bad as a play can be.

It was a failure, and I have not heard that many, either then or since, have denied that it was deservedly a failure. Johnson himself—"the anomalous Mr. Johnson," as Aaron Hill called him after seeing a performance of *Irene*—with his characteristic humour and sense, did not waste time in complaining of the verdict of the public. He had no sympathy with those authors who pay themselves in pomposity for what they lack in circulation. "To a thousand evils one answer is sufficient," he wrote of Pope's *Iliad*. "The purpose of a writer is to be read." He accepted the test both when it favoured him and when it did not.

He wrote for money, and he always agreed that, if one sought to sell a certain commodity to the public, then the public had the right to decide whether it wanted to buy or not. The public was his employer, "If an architect says, 'I will build five stories,' and the man who employs him says, 'I will have only three,' the employer," he says, "is to decide." Later, when a Mr. Pot was introduced to him as one who admired *Irene* as "the finest tragedy of modern times," Johnson was content to answer, "If Pot says so, Pot lies." When it was re-read to him in his old age, his only comment on it was, "Sir, I thought it had been better."

He had meanwhile turned his attention to a very different task. Encouraged by the promised patronage of Lord Chesterfield, he, in 1747, began to collect materials for a dictionary of the English language. It was his illusion that a language could be "fixed," and he proposed to give to the world a work in which once and for all the meaning of every English word would be authoritatively fixed. The task was one which, before it was finished, was to teach him many lessons, both about the nature of language and the nature of patrons.

Meanwhile the preparation of a dictionary may be an absorbing, but it is hardly a lucrative, employment. A married man had therefore to combine it with some other work which might be the provider of his daily bread. Johnson cast about in his mind to discover a form of writing which would be popular and yet would not require study or research. The answer—it is a curious commentary on mid-eighteenth-century taste—was the *Rambler*.

The *Rambler* appeared twice every week from March 20th, 1750, to March 17th, 1752. For it Johnson received two guineas a copy—not at all bad pay. It belonged to a family of which Addison's *Spectator* was the founder, and comparison of the two is perhaps inevitable. Yet though there is between them a similarity of form and thought the curiosity that both writers spent their boyhood in Lichfield may perhaps have tempted some critics to make as much as possible of that similarity, yet there is no real similarity either of content or between the minds of the two authors. Indeed, not Addison, but Sir Thomas Browne, has been hailed as Johnson's master. "The observation of his having imitated Sir Thomas Browne," writes Boswell, "has been made by many people; and lately it has been insisted on, and illustrated by a variety of quotations from Browne, in one of the popular essays written by the Reverend Mr. Knox." I do not think that the Reverend Mr.

Knox—in fact, the Reverend Mr. Vicesimus Knox, if one may call a spade a spade—entirely makes out his case. Yet, though Johnson admired Addison, claimed his to be "the model of the middle style," and wrote that "whoever wishes to attain an English style, familiar but not coarse and elegant but not ostentatious, must give his days and nights to the volumes of Addison," he was certainly to some extent in conscious reaction against the artificialities of Queen Anne's reign. The dainty but drunken Addison had neither the virtues nor the vices of Tory Samuel Johnson. If we would praise or blame the *Rambler*, we must do so for its own merits or defects.

It is curious to see the spirit in which Johnson undertook this work. A journalist is to write for money a series of hack-articles. Before sitting down to it, he first composes a prayer:

> "Almighty God, the giver of all good things, without Whose help all labour is ineffectual and without Whose grace all wisdom is folly, grant, I beseech Thee, that in this my undertaking Thy Holy Spirit may not be withheld from me but that I may promote Thy glory and the salvation both of myself and others; grant this, O Lord, for the sake of Jesus Christ. Amen."

What proportion of the turnovers in *The Times*, I wonder, are preceded by prayer?

Yet the essays are not especially theological. They are on every topic that happens to have come to the author's mind, and on every topic except that of art they contain much sound sense. The difficulties of matrimony and the problems of prostitution were both continually present to him. There is much, too, on his favourite theme of the vanity of all human things.

> "The controversy about the reality of external evils," he writes, "is now at end. That life has many miseries and that those miseries are sometimes at least equal to all the powers of fortitude is now universally confessed."

Perhaps there is in them sometimes too much of the pedagogue, and, when he tries to be humorous, too much of the elephant. Yet, when these two defects are granted, I am by no means ready to join in the modern chorus of their detraction. One critic complains that they are prosaic. The quality is not necessarily a defect in a piece of prose. It is often said that they are nothing but lay sermons. If so, at least they share the happy praise which Boswell gave to Ogden's *Second* and *Ninth Sermons on Prayer,* "which, with their other distinguished excellence, have the merit of being short." And if you can tell me of a living preacher whose sermons contain one half of the wisdom or one half of the goodness that I can find in the *Rambler,* I will be of that man's congregation every Sunday.

What sermon could have a wiser or a more necessary text, or one more wittily expressed, than that "unwillingness to be pleased is not necessarily a proof of understanding"? Or a nobler peroration than:

> "Of him that hopes to be forgiven it is indispensably required that he forgive. It is therefore superfluous to urge any other motive. On this great duty eternity is suspended; and to him that refuses to practise it the throne of mercy is inaccessible and the Saviour of the world has been born in vain"?

If one half of the æsthetic people who have sneered at the *Rambler* had instead read it and profited from it, how much happier a place the world would be!

If the *Rambler* be a volume of sermons, at least it is often La Rochefoucauld in the pulpit. "The fondest and firmest friendships are," in Johnson's opinion, "dissolved by such openness and sincerity as interrupt our enjoyment of our own approbation." And, among the causes of human misery he gave a larger place to envy of others' success than is, I believe and hope, justified.

Yet I do not deny the power of the *Rambler* to bore. Sometimes, too, Johnson's advice becomes almost ridiculous in its pomposity. When, for instance, he warns us "let no man from this time allow his felicity to depend on the death of his aunt," we can but feel, like one who suddenly stumbles across the prohibition of marriage with his grandmother in the "Table of Kindred and Affinity," that it was a temptation to which, even without such warnings, we were not normally likely to fall. To read a hundred and fifty *Ramblers* on end is uphill work. But all comparisons are relative. To read a hundred and fifty sermons on end would be impossible. Let us throw to the enemy the elephantine *Rambler,* the allegorical *Rambler,* the *Rambler* in parable. There is plenty left to us.

If it be the purpose of good prose—and it is its purpose, whatever an æsthetic prattle may say—to tell the truth as clearly as it can be told, then there are not many places where you will find better prose than that of the best *Ramblers.* They are not good prose as Ruskin or as Pater wrote it, nor yet as Voltaire wrote or as M. Maurras writes it. Johnson neither debates nor adorns. Yet he says what he has to say clearly and well—that is, he writes good prose.

Sir Walter Raleigh has selected for especial praise the end of the essay on "Bashfulness":

> "No cause more frequently produces bashfulness than too high an opinion of our own importance. He that imagines an assembly filled with his merit, panting with expectation and hushed with attention, easily terrifies himself with the dread of disappointing them and strains his imagination in pursuit of something that may vindicate the veracity of fame and show that his reputation was not gained by chance. He considers that what he shall say or do will never be forgotten; that renown or infamy is suspended upon every syllable

Portrait of Mrs. Thrale, afterwards Mrs. Piozzi
after a picture by Sir Joshua Reynolds

and that nothing ought to fall from him which will not bear the test of time. Under such solicitude who can wonder that the mind is overwhelmed and, by struggling with attempts above her strength, quickly sinks into languishment and despondency?

"The most useful medicines are often unpleasing to the taste. Those who are oppressed by their own reputation will perhaps not be comforted by hearing that their fears are unnecessary. But the truth is that no man is much regarded by the rest of the world. He that considers how little he dwells upon the condition of others will learn how little the attention of others is attracted by himself. While we see multitudes passing before us of whom perhaps not one appears to deserve our notice or excite our sympathy, we should remember that we likewise are lost in the same throng; that the eye which happens to glance upon us is turned in a moment on him that follows us and that the utmost we can reasonably hope or fear is to fill a vacant hour with prattle and be forgotten."

This is wise writing. Set beside it an extract from the essay on "The Narrowness of Human Fame." After saying how very few are they who have intellectual curiosity at all, Johnson goes on:

"Even of those who have dedicated themselves to knowledge the far greater part have confined their curiosity to a few objects and have very little inclination to promote any fame but that which their own studies entitle them to partake. The naturalist has no desire to know the opinions or conjectures of the philologist; the botanist looks upon the astronomer as a being unworthy of his regard; the lawyer scarcely hears the name of a physician without contempt; and he that is growing great and happy by electrifying a bottle wonders how the world can be engaged by trifling prattle about war or peace.

"If therefore he that imagines the world filled with his actions and praises shall subduct from the number of his encomiasts all those who are placed below the flight of fame and who hear in the valleys of life no voice but that of necessity; all those who imagine themselves too important to regard him and consider the mention of his name as a usurpation of their time; all who are too much or too little pleased with themselves to attend to anything external; all who are attracted by pleasure, or chained down by pain, to unvaried ideas; all who are withheld from attending his triumph by different pursuits; and all who slumber in universal negligence; he will find his renown straitened by nearer bounds than the rocks of Caucasus and perceive that no man can be venerable or formidable but to a small part of his fellow-creatures."

Open your *Rambler* at random. You will easily find other passages as wise, as true and as lucid.

You will find—I do not doubt—no original truth, in the sense that there is nothing here being said for the first time in human history. Such originality Johnson did not at all possess. It was an originality of which he would have been both suspicious and contemptuous. But originality, in the sense that what he said came from his origins, he did possess. He is not merely handing on as a writer the lesson which he learnt yesterday as a reader. The truth is his own truth. He has discovered it for himself and the discovery has been none the less real if other wise men have made it before him.

Three days after the appearance of the last *Rambler* Mrs. Johnson died. The difference in age between the couple had been so great, the appearance and manners of both so unusual, that, as long as Mrs. Johnson survived, it had been difficult to think of their married life without ridicule. And Johnson, a porpoise in bed, made what would anyhow have been ridiculous more ridiculous still. Yet at her death the laughter of ridicule was rebuked. Johnson loved where a man of smaller heart could not have loved; where, as has been hinted, even a man of keener eyesight could not have loved; and few of the world's loveliest and best have been mourned as that old, painted harridan, Tetty Johnson, was mourned. Johnson was heart-broken at his loss, and, even after thirty years, we still find him sadly and religiously marking the day of her death. That day, with New Year's Day, Good Friday, and his birthday, was every year set apart by him for fasting and prayer.

For the moment he found refuge from his grief where alone, I suppose, refuge can be found—in hard work.

> "O Lord, our Heavenly Father," he prayed, "without Whom all purposes are frustrate, all efforts are vain, grant me the assistance of Thy Holy Spirit that I may not sorrow as one without hope but may now return to the duties of my present state with humble confidence in Thy protection, and so govern my thoughts and actions that neither business may withdraw my mind from Thee nor idleness lay me open to vain imaginations; that neither praise may fill me with pride nor censure with discontent; but that in the changes of this life I may fix my heart upon the reward which Thou hast promised to them that serve Thee, and that whatever things are true, whatever things are honest, whatever things are just, whatever are pure, whatever are lovely, whatever are of good report, wherein there is virtue, wherein there is praise, I may think upon and do, and obtain mercy and everlasting happiness. Grant this, O Lord, for the sake of Jesus Christ. Amen."

Yet hard work was not natural to him, for his mind was too full to need that escape from himself which the output of energy gives. But now his own company was too sad. No longer did he need money in order to support a wife but the blockhead had found another motive than money from which to write. In order to escape from himself he must express himself. The dictionary was hurried on.

By the beginning of 1755 it was almost ready for the press. The first plan of it had been dedicated to Lord Chesterfield, the greatest of the literary patrons of the day. Yet during the long years of preparation Chesterfield had not bothered himself to give any assistance to the struggling author. Now that the work seemed about to appear, he became ambitious that his name should be upon its title-page.

He wrote a couple of ostentatious "puffs" on Johnson in the *World*. Johnson was not to be so easily fooled, and he replied to Chesterfield in a letter which is, I suppose, the world's masterpiece of dignified rebuke.

"TO THE RIGHT HONOURABLE
THE EARL OF CHESTERFIELD.

"February 7th, 1755.

"MY LORD,—I have lately been informed by the proprietor of the *World* that two papers in which my Dictionary was recommended to the public were written by your Lordship. To be so distinguished is an honour which, being very little accustomed to favours from the great, I know not well how to receive nor in what terms to acknowledge.

"When, upon some slight encouragement, I first

visited your Lordship, I was overpowered, like the rest of mankind, by the enchantment of your address and could not forbear to wish that I might boast myself *le vainqueur du vainqueur de la terre;* that I might obtain that regard for which I saw the world contending; but I found my attendance so little encouraged that neither pride nor modesty would suffer me to continue it. When I had once addressed your Lordship in public I had exhausted all the art of pleasing which a retired and uncourtly scholar can possess. I had done all that I could; and no man is well pleased to have his all neglected, be it ever so little.

"Seven years, my Lord, have now passed since I waited in your outward rooms or was repulsed from your door; during which time I have been pushing on my work through difficulties of which it is useless to complain and have brought it at last to the verge of publication, without one act of assistance, one word of encouragement or one smile of favour. Such treatment I did not expect, for I never had a Patron before.

"The shepherd in Virgil grew at last acquainted with Love and found him a native of the rocks.

"Is not a Patron, my Lord, one who looks with unconcern on a man struggling for life in the water and, when he has reached ground, encumbers him with help? The notice which you have been pleased to take of my work, had it been early, had been kind; but it has been delayed till I am indifferent and cannot enjoy it; till I am solitary and cannot impart it; till I am known and do not want it. I hope it is no very cynical asperity not to confess obligations where no benefit has been received, or to be unwilling that the public should consider me as owing to a Patron that which Providence has enabled me to do for myself.

"Having carried on my work thus far with so little obligation to any favourer of learning, I shall not be disappointed though I should conclude it, if less be possible, with less; for I have been long wakened from that dream of hope in which I once boasted myself with so much exultation, my Lord, Your Lordship's most humble, most obedient servant,

"SAM. JOHNSON.

Everyone has praised this letter, and everyone has praised it for a different reason—which is, I suppose, a test of greatness. Each re-reading shows some new thing to admire in the offensiveness of the phrasing. How masterly is the device by which he avoids paying that insincere compliment with which it is customary to close a letter!

And yet what was Johnson's grievance against Lord Chesterfield? Chesterfield was, it is true, at the bottom of his soul a crude bounder. His letters show that. Yet he was a man of some kindness and of some cynical wisdom. He foresaw and prophesied a French revolution. Curiously enough, his and

Johnson's are two of the very few voices raised in protest against the barbarity of eighteenth-century English rule in Ireland. Justice has been done to him with posterity neither by Johnson nor by Dickens, who is said to have put him into *Barnaby Rudge* as the elder Chester and who, if so, wholly misunderstood his character. Chesterfield gave his life to the vulgarities of the world; at least he never made before them the ultimate surrender of believing in them.

It is also a little difficult to see in what way he had violated the conventional code of patrons' morals. That code, it is true, was not an heroic one, but Johnson had sufficient of the wisdom of the world not to expect to find heroism in so strange a place. "If virtuous authors must be patronised only by virtuous peers, who shall point them out?" he asks in his *Life of Young*, appropriately leaving it uncertain to whom the "them" refers. "Such treatment I did not expect." What treatment did he expect?

He does not seem to have suffered any direct repulse—at least, any direct repulse of which Chesterfield was personally guilty. Rather he gradually passed out of Chesterfield's life in the way in which we all inevitably allow acquaintances to pass out of our lives. Johnson was too proud to force the continuance of the relationship, and it was not, it is probable, until Chesterfield heard Johnson talked about, owing to the approaching appearance of the dictionary, that it fully struck him that he had dropped his protégé.

Yet the answer is, I suppose, that Chesterfield was rich and Johnson was not. Some envy the rich; others sponge on them; but very few, as the rich themselves well know, really like them. Chesterfield was not perhaps personally insolent, yet there is a necessary insolence in the relationship of the rich with those who are not of them which to a sensitive man such as Johnson was intolerable.

Much nonsense is talked against the system of patronage. That an author should have had to depend for his living upon the favours of Lord Chesterfield was certainly an evil. Yet he who will live like Samuel Johnson is rare; and if a man must live by flattery, which is the worse—he who lives by flattering Lord Chesterfield or he who lives by flattering Middle Western women's clubs? Let the modern author who is quite indifferent to his American sales cast the first stone at eighteenth-century patronage. Under our present conditions of mass-flattery, a La Rochefoucauld would be an impossibility, and the world is greatly the loser.

In 1755 the dictionary came out. When the last sheet was taken to Millar, the publisher, Johnson asked the messenger if Millar had made any comment.

"Sir," said the messenger, "he said, 'Thank God I have done with him.' "

"I am glad," said Johnson, "that he thanks God for anything."

Two or three of Johnson's definitions everybody

knows—his blunders on "pastern" and "windward," the definition of an exciseman, of oats, of a lexicographer, and so on. Of the letter "H," he strangely observed that it "seldom, perhaps never, begins any but the first syllable!" Wilkes wittily commented, "The author of this observation must be a man of quick apprehension and of a most comprehensive genius." Only his impeccable manners can have prevented him from calling Johnson a "blockhead."

The serious qualities of the dictionary are to-day less known and less appreciated. Nor in the era of Murray is there much reason why they should be known to any except the scholar. Johnson deserves the pioneer's praise. Yet those who have come after him have used him and superseded him. In any case there would doubtless have been progress, and, as it was, there were in Johnson two defects which made it very necessary that his work should be superseded. He set out to "fix" the English language. Long before his task was finished he had gained sense to see the impossibility of his ambition. The task was, in its nature, impossible. Even had it been possible to nature, it would not have been possible to Johnson, for he was no etymologist and, while he knew his Shakespeare and Ben Jonson, he was but imperfectly acquainted with the rest of Elizabethan literature—two large handicaps.

It was one of his peccadilloes to refuse to confess to the second of these handicaps. Knowledge and ignorance are doubtless relative. Yet, whatever he may have claimed, the scarcity of quotation from other Elizabethan authors prove that their works were not his familiar companions and his remarks about Elizabethan society in the Preface to his edition of Shakespeare show how little was his understanding of it. "Mr. Hume said"—to Boswell—"that he would give me half a crown for every page of his"—Johnson's—"dictionary in which he could not find an absurdity if I would give him half a crown for every page in which he did find one."

Yet, even though the task was not perfectly performed, Johnson deserves praise for the industry which enabled him to perform it at all. He had, it is true, secretaries. Yet substantially he had, as he liked to be told, done alone for the English language what it had taken all the French Academy to do for the French. It established him in that position which he was to hold for the rest of his life—the position of "great Cham of literature."

He had gained the respect of all men. Yet respect is a dangerous advantage. On the one hand the deference of others vastly increases the pleasures of idleness, and yet respect is of itself of little, if any, financial advantage. If anything, it makes people vaguely imagine that you have an independent income.

To Johnson its temptations were fatal. He produced during these years the *Idler*—a second *Rambler*. But the main task which he had set himself was that of an edition of Shakespeare, for which he had received, pocketed, and spent subscriptions. Yet the book tarried unconscionably for nine years.

Johnson had unfortunately once pronounced Churchill, the satirist, to be "a shallow fellow." Johnson's dilatoriness gave Churchill his opportunity, and in his poem, the *Ghost,* he pilloried him as Dom Pomposo. In six stinging lines he openly accused him of financial fraud.

> He for subscribers baits his hook,
> And takes your cash; but where's the book?
> No matter where; wise fear, you know,
> Forbids the robbing of a foe;
> But what, to serve our private ends,
> Forbids the cheating of our friends?

In 1756 Richardson had had to lend Johnson six guineas in order to release him from arrest for debt. The lexicographer's begging letter is a pathetic business.

"SIR,—I am obliged to entreat your assistance. I am now under an arrest for five pounds eighteen shillings. Mr. Strahan, from whom I should have received the necessary help in this case, is not at home; and I am afraid of not finding Mr. Millar. If you will be so good as to send me this sum I will very gratefully repay you and add it to all former obligations. I am, Sir,

"Your most obedient
"and most humble servant,
"SAMUEL JOHNSON.

"GOUGH SQUARE, 16 *March.*"

Even such necessity was not able to stir him. "A kind of strange oblivion has spread over me so that I know not what has become of the last years," he wrote in 1764.

Yet during those years there had fallen upon him a new sorrow. In 1759 his mother had died. His relations with her had been peculiar. He had loved her, as he said with his usual passion for drawing distinctions, but had not respected her. "One day when in anger she called me a puppy I asked her if she knew what they called a puppy's mother," Mrs. Piozzi quotes Johnson as telling her, and was attacked for doing so—perhaps with justice—by Peter Pindar.

> Who, mad'ning with an anecdotic itch,
> Declared that Johnson called his mother B—TCH?

Yet Johnson does not seem to have been ashamed of the story. If he had been he need not have repeated it. Nevertheless, although he had not seen her for some years, he was deeply affected at his mother's death. Still such bereavements are in nature and this one would not be worth recalling were it not that, in order to pay some debts which she had left, he wrote, in the evenings of one week, *Rasselas,* in some ways the most interesting of all his works.

The story of *Rasselas* is that of a young prince of Abyssinia who, brought up in a secluded Happy Valley, becomes discontented with the dullness of his life, and, in company with the philosopher, Imlac, sallies out into the world, meets with various adventures and various people and learns, as one would expect a Johnsonian character to learn, that there is little happiness to be found anywhere and that one station and one place are much the same as another. He returns therefore to Abyssinia.

In *Rasselas* comes Johnson's curious prophecy of flying. Perhaps, too, it shows him at his best in his use of the antithetical style. Take for instance the saying of the astronomer, "To man is permitted the contemplation of the skies, but the practice of virtue is commanded." The distinction, though true and important, is doubtless not original. Indeed, Johnson himself makes it again when, in his *Life of Milton,* he says, "We are perpetually moralists, but we are geometricians only by chance." Yet it could not have been more neatly put. It is a lesson for every schoolmaster. *Rasselas* contains, too, much sound political advice and should be studied by all whose enthusiasm is inclined to destroy their sense of proportion. Take that great mixture of cynicism and wisdom in which Imlac lays down his political philosophy.

> "Sir," said Imlac, "your ardour is the natural effect of virtue animated by youth: the time will come when you will acquit your father and perhaps hear with less impatience of the governor. Oppression is in the Abissinian dominions neither frequent nor tolerated: but no form of government

has yet been discovered by which cruelty can be wholly prevented. Subordination supposes power on one part and subjection on the other; and if power be in the hands of men it will sometimes be abused. The vigilance of the supreme magistrate may do much, but much will still remain undone. He can never know all the crimes that are committed, and can seldom punish all that he knows."

A few days before its publication appeared Voltaire's *Candide.* Between the two works is some similarity. In *Candide* a Westphalian gentleman wanders over the world in search of happiness, as Rasselas wanders over the world in Johnson's book. There is a philosopher, Dr. Pangloss, as there is a philosopher, Imlac, in *Rasselas.* Both Rasselas and Candide fail in their quests. From these resemblances it has been argued that Johnson must have at least heard of *Candide* and Johnson's denial has been necessary in order to save him from the suspicion of plagiarism.

It is hard to see how any can have made such a charge, even though Johnson himself thought that there was a similarity in the two books. *Candide* was a work written in answer to Rousseau's complaints of Voltaire's alleged atheism. The Rousseauan argument was that man was good (though corrupted by institutions), and that therefore the God Who made him must be good. To refute, or, rather, to satirise, the first step in that argument *Candide* was written.

It is a task into which any man with a certain zest for baseness would wade eagerly. Such a zest Voltaire certainly had. Even his noblest humanitarian tirades are often, one cannot but feel, inspired more by hatred of the judge than by love of the prisoner. And, if we remember that the book was admittedly a satire, it is unfair to object that even this wretched world is not peopled by cads quite so impossible as those into whose clutches, one after another, Candide is made to fall. The Rousseauans had been responsible for the generalisation that man was good. It was a fair refutation of that generalisation to produce individuals who were bad and to show that their existence was not inconceivable.

At the same time one cannot help noting, if only for amusement, all the familiar Voltairean formulæ. When Dr. Pangloss has to be stricken with a venereal disease, it has to be explained that a Jesuit formed one link in the chain by which the disease descended to him from a sailor of Christopher Columbus. An illegitimate child inevitably discovers the Pope to be her father. When, for relief, one decent character is introduced, he is made to be an anabaptist. No one wishes to hold an extravagant brief for the Churchmen of the eighteenth century. Still, even in the eighteenth century Jesuits were not the only people who infected others with diseases, nor did popes alone beget illegitimate daughters. The Christian virtues were not the quite exclusive monopoly of people outside the Christian Church.

Yet in excuse for Voltaire it must be remembered how much weaker was the intellectual defence of the Christian faith in the France of his day than it is to-day. The Church in France was, in his lifetime, "under the water," to quote Mr. Belloc's phrase. Voltaire himself was a man of no historical imagination. He was unable to realise that there had ever been a time when her rôle was very different from that played by the Gallicanised emasculation which had survived from the triumphs of Louis XIV. Nor was he a metaphysician. By consequence it was never driven into his mind that the Christian religion possessed a metaphysic as well as an organisation. To point out that there were a lot of bad priests—as there certainly were—and to make a joke or two about Habakkuk were, he thought, all that was necessary for its demolition.

Yet to raise these objections is merely to say that the book is by Voltaire. And to say that is to say that it will certainly suffer from his faults and as certainly possess also his merits. Of these the largest are memorableness and lucidity. One may contrast the two books by saying that *Rasselas* contains much more that is worth remembering and *Candide* much more that one does remember.

Candide is, as I have said, a satire. The incidents in it are therefore purposely exaggerated and impossible. The object of *Rasselas* is different. Johnson has no especial thesis of another to refute. He merely wishes to show that man's search after happiness is not normally successful. Rasselas therefore is made to fall into the company of people exaggeratedly going about their ordinary business. This is a difference which gives an entirely different nature to the two works.

That Johnson would have been on the side of Voltaire in his controversy with Rousseau is certain. Himself, in his essay on those doctrines which Soame Jenyns had copied from Pope, he has refuted a similar, if not exactly the same, optimism. Indeed, it is hard to imagine a sane man who really thought that the goodness of God was to be deduced from the goodness of this world nor would it be easy to find at all a wise one who did not agree that in this world, if you looked at it as an end, there was a great deal more pain than pleasure. Doubtless

> God's in His heaven;
> All's right with the world.

The sane man argues that, because "God's in His heaven," therefore we must believe that, ultimately and incomprehensibly, "all's right with the world." The fool argues that "all's right with the world," and therefore "God's in His heaven."

Johnson believed in the goodness of God for a reason purely metaphysical. Evil was a privation of good, and therefore a limitation. It was, then, a contradiction in terms to speak of a Being unlimited but evil. God was good "because of the absence of any reason for His being other"—not because, but in spite, of this world. The evils of the world were very real and very terrible, but they were no reason for abandoning faith in God. Cancer was a great evil, but you did not cure yourself of cancer by becoming an atheist.

Johnson then differed from Rousseau radically. From Voltaire he only differed in so far as Voltaire stopped short at his refutation of Rousseau, imagining that he had refuted all that there was to refute. For Candide has never really sought for happiness at all; he has merely sought for sensation. And Voltaire's work proves, if it proves anything, that the mere searcher after sensation can never attain to satisfaction—which is a truth, but a very small truth.

Johnson knew well all that Voltaire knew. Life at the best was an affair of very great sadness. Life, if the consolations of religion were a cheat, was an unfaceable evil. If this impermanence is all, what is life but a melancholy record of loved things lost and loved friends lost? What sane ambition can a man have in it save the ambition to predecease those for whom he cares?

> "Piety is the only proper and adequate relief of decaying man. He that grows old without religious hopes, as he declines into imbecility and feels pains and sorrows crowding upon him, falls into a gulf of bottomless miseries in which every reflection must plunge him deeper and where he

finds only new gradations of anguish and precipices of horror."

Yet Johnson differed from Voltaire because his criticism was not merely destructive. For he knew that there was a certain satisfaction of the reason which was not, as are the sensual pleasures, wholly at the mercy of change and chance. In that satisfaction it was open to man to find some refuge from unhappiness. Yet his pessimism was not therefore destroyed. For he knew well how very few did truly make their escape even among those who professed to do so. The world was too much with them and, as long as the world was with them, they could not be happy.

This is the lesson of the last and best chapter of *Rasselas*. Each of the characters has by then discovered that only in a life of reason can happiness be found. Yet the nature of man forbids him from complete indifference to the material environment in which he can exercise his reason, and that appropriate material environment the philosopher, only too frequently, is unable to obtain. Such is the conclusion of *Rasselas*.

"The Conclusion in which Nothing is Concluded

"It was now the time of the inundation of the Nile: a few days after their visit to the catacombs the river began to rise.

"They were confined to their house. The whole region being under water gave them no invitation to any excursions and, being well supplied with materials for talk, they diverted themselves with comparisons of the different forms of life which they had observed and with various schemes of happiness which each of them had formed.

"Pekuah was never so charmed with any place as the convent of St. Antony where the Arab restored her to the Princess, and wished only to fill it with pious maidens and to be made prioress of the order: she was weary of expectation and disgust and would gladly be fixed in some invariable state.

"The Princess thought that of all sublunary things knowledge was the best: she desired first to learn all sciences and then purposed to found a college of learned women in which she would preside, that, by conversing with the old and educating the young, she might divide her time between the acquisition and communication of wisdom and raise up for the next age models of prudence and patterns of piety.

"The Prince desired a little kingdom in which he might administer justice in his own person and see all the parts of government with his own eyes; but he could never fix the limits of his dominions and was always adding to the number of his subjects.

"Imlac and the Astronomer were contented to

be driven along the stream of life without directing their course to any particular port.

"Of these wishes that they had formed they knew that none could be obtained. They deliberated awhile what was to be done and resolved when the inundation should cease to return to Abissinia."

In the railing against God of a Victor Hugo is something childish and vulgar. The unrelieved blackness which at times filled the great minds of Shakespeare and of Swift is terrifying and almost lunatic. But to understand that external goods benefit us not at all unless we have the knack of using them so as to bring us happiness, and not therefore to complain if we lose happiness through our own folly—this, platitudinous as it is, is about all the teaching on this world which wise philosophy can give us. Socrates, before his accusing judges, gave it to us two thousand years ago—"Sir, when a man knows he is to be hanged in a fortnight it concentrates his mind wonderfully"—and Johnson gave it to us again in the fading twilight of the *ancien régime.*

Nor at the end need we exclude Voltaire from the company of Johnson and Socrates. For he, too, comes at last to the conclusion that *"il faut cultiver notre jardin"* and *"après tout, c'est un monde passable."* The world of Johnson and of Voltaire is as irrevocably gone as is that of Socrates. Voltaire has won, but, conquering Johnson, he has been beaten by his own disciples. The power of the priests has been broken. To-day they gain a little here and lose a little there, but there is no human sign of a large revival. In its place has come a power more alien to the loves and the passion for justice of Voltaire's great mind than any that he ever knew or denounced. With all his faults, Voltaire had in him a very noble hatred—the hatred for the insolence of the powerful man who thinks that his power sets him free from the moral law. Yet this hatred, though very noble, was, on his philosophy, very illogical. Voltaire preached to the poor that the hell by fear of which the rich man kept them in slavery was but a fairy-tale—and the rich man heard about it. He went away rejoicing, for he had great possessions. If hell was a lie, there need be no more of this sentimental pother about selling all that he had.

Convention demands that we go out to dine, and that we ask one another, "What do you think about this?" and "What do you think about that?" Yet we know very well that the truth is that very few of us think about such things at all. We like to be heard saying—which is a very different affair. People whose intelligence is quite unequal to following the method of scoring points for the county cricket championship, yet imagine that they have the right, by an unconsidered *ipse dixit* delivered over a whisky-and-soda, to settle problems of which the genius of Socrates knew after a lifetime only that he knew nothing and which baffled impartially the subtlety of Pascal and the lucidity of Calvin. Yet, scattered through history, there have been a few men who have really taken their opinions seriously. Such men have not always thought right; at least they have always thought. When they have claimed to think this or that about a thing, at least they have really thought about it. Of such a company was Voltaire. Of such a company was Johnson.

Voltaire was a rationalist, in the sense in which Johnson or Huxley or St. Thomas Aquinas were rationalists, in the only sense in which that noble word should ever be used. That is to say, he was a man who, if you proved to him that a certain conclusion would follow from his premises, was willing to accept that conclusion. When he lied, as he did in the *Pucelle,* he knew that he lied and did it deliberately to give pain.

Much that calls itself Reason is really only smallness of imagination. Faith is the gift of God which enables us to make our will accept the conclusion of our Reason. A faith, then, which sets itself up in opposition to Reason, if the word "Reason" be rightly used, is a fool's faith. For how can a man submit his Reason? What has he but his Reason—his "Monarch Reason," in the fine and important phrase of Dryden—which can command him to submit? By Reason let us judge the dispute of Johnson and Voltaire.

In logic, rationalism is, I admit, not incompatible

with infidelity. Voltaire proved that in his own day, and such thinkers as Dean Inge or Professor Santayana prove it in ours. Yet, except in a few sad survivors of Huxley who live on into an age which they do not know and do not care to know, rationalism and infidelity are to-day divorced. Voltaire attacked the Christian faith because, as he maintained, it offended Reason. The modern sceptic is apt to admit that logic is on the side of the faith but to plead that life is larger than logic. The attack on religion to-day is becoming more and more but one aspect of that general attack on Reason which is so dangerously rife in every country of Western Europe and by which the civilisation of Western Europe is so desperately menaced. That attack is an attack on Voltaire every bit as much as on *l'infâme,* an attack on Voltaire every bit as much as on Samuel Johnson.

Each generation has its fashionable heresy and the fashionable exponent of that heresy who is lucky enough to have the happy knack of giving to his contemporaries reasons for doing and believing the things that they want to do and believe. He gains his popularity because, in the brilliant, if brutal, phrase of Charles II, "his nonsense suits their nonsense." Such a man was Voltaire. Yet, though he bowed the knee to nonsense, he at least never worshipped confessedly in the temple of unreason.

Irrationalism is a dangerous enemy because it is always trying to steal on to its side the servants of Reason. In the age that followed that of Johnson and Voltaire hardly anyone set himself up more whole-heartedly as the apostle of unreason and of the revolt of the barbarian than did Carlyle, and no better example could be found of the rhetorician's subtle tactics than that of Carlyle's essay on Johnson.

For the merits of that essay it is right to be grateful. Carlyle rehabilitated Boswell from Macaulay's monstrous paradox, truly insisting that evil is but negative and could never have produced a good book or, indeed, any good thing. He also praised Johnson, even where he could least understand him. Yet Carlyle's praise is often more dangerous than another's blame. He praises Johnson as if he were some half-witted, strong, silent German idealist, a "Ruler-Soul," a "King," a "Believer," a "Man." He marvels "how Samuel Johnson, in the era of Voltaire, can purify and fortify his soul and hold real communion with the Highest in the Church of St. Clement Danes."

What sad, overcoloured nonsense this is! Johnson was a believer and went to church—and that was a very sensible thing to have done. But, to read Carlyle, one might think that going to church in the age of Voltaire was an act as heroic as going to church in the age of Nero, that Johnson was the last, faithful worshipper at some old and forgotten shrine. Yet, in Johnson's England, though it was a country of much worldliness and some infidelity, the overwhelming majority of the people believed in some form or other of the Christian religion and the majority probably attended some place of Christian worship most Sundays of their lives. It is as if one were to congratulate a man on eating a chop "in the era of Eustace Miles." How amused, we may be sure, Johnson would have been to hear of this fantastic fuss about a normal Englishman performing the normal obligation of a Christian!

The passage is a good example of what I mean when I say that Carlyle was the enemy of Reason. Like the rest of us, he was sometimes right and sometimes wrong. But, when he was right, when Reason was on his side, the whole effort of his style was to keep the shameful secret as dark as possible. Carlyle was for Rhetoric against Reason; Johnson, more than any man that ever lived, for Reason against Rhetoric. Carlyle praised Johnson, but he was but ill fitted to do so; for Johnson cannot be properly praised by a sentimentalist. Only Reason can praise Reason.

Voltaire, Johnson, and Chesterfield then, with all their differences, yet up to a point approached life in the same way. They stood together both against the optimism of Rousseau and against the irrationalism which Carlyle was afterwards to preach. The world was full of evils—"problems," Chesterfield would perhaps have preferred as the less vulgar word—of whose existence it was a waste of time to complain, against which it was a futility to rant and which only Reason could at all arm us to meet.

Yet Johnson was a deeper thinker than either of

the other two. For neither of them ever asked why there should be this evil in the world. Leslie Stephen says that Johnson did not ask it either. Yet this is untrue. He asked it and answered it; and, because he did so, he is a greater man than Voltaire.

The easiest answer is to say that evil exists because God, if there be a God, does not greatly bother Himself with the comfort of that very petty thing, the human race. The only other answer is the Christian answer. This answer Johnson gives in an essay in the *Adventurer*.

If it be true that heaven alone can give us happiness and that this life is but a testing-ground, then certainly a man is robbing himself so far as he concentrates his attention upon the passing goods of this world to the exclusion of the ultimate good. He is continually grasping at a happiness which continually eludes him. Yet the pleasure even of such a world as this engrosses most men almost exclusively. Had God created for us, as of course He could have created, a lotus-eaters' world where there was neither pain nor labour nor storm, what man would there have been found with strength to look beyond that world to the true source of happiness? "Prosperity," says Johnson, "alloyed and imperfect as it is, has power to intoxicate the imagination, to fix the mind upon the present scene, to produce confidence and elation and to make him who enjoys affluence and honours forget the hand by which they are bestowed." And again: "If our present state were one continued succession of delights, or one uniform flow of calmness and tranquillity, we should never willingly think upon its end; death would then surely surprise us 'as a thief in the night.'" The sorrows of this world, like the physical pains of purgatory or the possibility of the physical pains of hell, come not from the wrath of God, but from His mercy.

On poor Soame Jenyns, who tried to explain evil on a theory of Calibanism, Johnson was deliciously amusing. Just as we kill animals, there were, thought Jenyns, superior beings "who deceive, torment and destroy us for the ends only of their own pleasure or utility."

> "I cannot resist the temptation of contemplating this analogy which I think he might have carried further very much to the advantage of his argument. He might have shown that these 'hunters whose game is man' have many sports analogous to our own. As we drown whelps and kittens they amuse themselves now and then with sinking a ship, and stand round the fields of Blenheim or the walls of Prague, as we encircle a cockpit. As we shoot a bird flying they take a man in the midst of his business or pleasure and knock him down with an apoplexy. Some of them perhaps are virtuosi and delight in the operations of an asthma, as a human philosopher in the effects of the air-pump. To swell a man with tympany is as good a sport as to blow a frog. Many a merry bout have these

frolic beings at the vicissitudes of an ague, and good sport it is to see a man tumble with an epilepsy and revive and tumble again and all this he knows not why. As they are wiser and more powerful than we, they have more exquisite diversions, for we have no way of procuring any sport so brisk and so lasting as the paroxysms of the gout and stone which undoubtedly must make high mirth, especially if the play be a little diversified with the blunders and puzzles of the blind and deaf. We know not how far their sphere of observation may extend. Perhaps now and then a merry being may place himself in such a situation as to enjoy at once all the varieties of an epidemical disease or amuse his leisure with the tossings and contortions of every possible pain exhibited together.

"One sport the merry malice of these beings has found means of enjoying to which we have nothing equal or similar. They now and then catch a mortal proud of his parts and flattered either by the submission of those who court his kindness or the notice of those who suffer him to court theirs. A head thus prepared for the reception of false opinions and the projections of vain designs, they easily fill with idle notions till in time they make their plaything an author: their first diversion commonly begins with an ode or an epistle, then rises perhaps to a political irony and is at last brought to its height by a treatise of philosophy. Then begins the poor animal to entangle himself in sophisms and flounder in absurdity, to talk confidently of the scale of being and to give solutions which himself confesses impossible to be understood. Sometimes however it happens that their pleasure is without much mischief. The author feels no pain but, while they are wondering at the extravagance of his opinion and pointing him out to one another as a new example of human folly, he is enjoying his own applause and that of his companions and perhaps is elevated with the hope of standing at the head of a new sect.

"Many of the books which now crowd the world may be justly suspected to be written for the sake of some invisible order of beings, for surely they are of no use to the corporeal inhabitants of the world. Of the productions of the last bounteous year how many can be said to serve any purpose of use or pleasure? The only end of writing is to enable the readers better to enjoy life or better to endure it: and how will either of these be put more in our power by him who tells us that we are puppets of which some creature not much wiser than ourselves manages the wires? That a set of beings unseen and unheard are hovering about us, trying experiments upon our sensibility, putting us in agony to see our limbs quiver, torturing us to madness that they may laugh at our vagaries, sometimes obstructing the bile that they may see how a man looks when he is yellow; sometimes breaking a traveller's bones to try how he will get home; sometimes wasting a man to a skeleton and sometimes killing him fat for the greater elegance of his hide."

In a similar style does Johnson deal with the theology of Pope's *Essay on Man.* And, indeed, Bolingbroke's deism, from which both Pope and Jenyns derived, was a very strange business. Peers who make a hobby of theology are not apt to contribute to human knowledge. This deism accepted without question what is surely by far the hardest of the Christian doctrines—that of the benevolence of God towards man—and yet rejected all the others which, once that is accepted, become by comparison simple.

If God wishes well towards man, then, on the arguments, say, of St. Anselm's *Cur Deus Homo* or Browning's *Saul,* something of the nature of the Incarnation does not appear improbable. If an Incarnation is to be expected, then it is not hard to believe the claims of our Lord to be Incarnate God; and, if He was God, why is it incredible that He would found a Church?

There are, I know, difficulties which have to be faced at each of these stages of the argument, but they are surely nothing to the difficulty of the first stage. When our laughter at Jenyns and his supermen has died down, we cannot but stop to wonder whether after all he may not possibly be right;

Sir
I did not care to detain your servant while I wrote an answer to your
letter, in which you seem to insinuate that I had promised more than I
am ready to perform. If I have raised your expectations by any thing that may
have escaped my memory I am sorry, and if you remind me of it shall thank
you for the favour. If I made fewer alterations than usual in the debates
it was only because there appear'd, and still appears to me to be less need
of alteration. As to Father Paul, I have not yet been just to my proposal,
but have met with impediments which I hope, are now at an end, and
if you find the progress hereafter not such as you have a right to expect
you can easily stimulate a negligent translator. I am Sir

Your humble servant
Sam: Johnson
Wednesday.

To Mr Cave at
St John's Gate

A facsimile of Johnson's handwriting

whether, even if there is little evidence that he is right, there is not as little evidence that he is wrong.

Since evil is a limitation, an unlimited Being must certainly be good. It is not possible to hold a very serious brief for the theology of either *Caliban upon Setebos* or for that of the Epicureans. In a sense certainly God must be good, but it may surely be in a sense that is profoundly inconvenient to the human race. The good God may be a person very different from the genial peasant woman's *bon Dieu,* always pulling His silly children out of the scrapes in which they have landed themselves. God is absolutely good in respect of Himself; but, if it be admitted, as it cannot but be admitted, that it is possible for any suffering, however small, whether in this world or in another, to come to any of His creatures, then He is not absolutely good in respect of the creature.

I suffer. You tell me that my suffering is for my ultimate good. It may be so. It does not affect the argument. For I say that a God Who leads me to good through evil is not a God Who is absolutely good in respect of me. It is nothing to the argument that my suffering may be the result of my misuse of my own freedom. I did not ask for freedom. Freedom is not my end; happiness is my end. Free beings may be to the greater glory of God but they are not to the greater happiness of the beings themselves.

"Partial evil," you tell me, "universal good"—and

doubtless you are right. But what is the universe? What comfort is that to me if I am but a part? And why should man be the crown of God's creation? Why should not Jenyns' supermen exist, and man exist only for their sport?

If any suffering at all is compatible with the goodness of God, why is not infinite suffering for the whole human race compatible with that goodness? There is no reason why all human history should not be but a little episode in God's great scheme, doubtless contributing to good and to God's glory on the whole, but in itself evil. The good God Who has destroyed the brontosaurus may also destroy the *homo sapiens*.

Once the truth of the Incarnation is admitted—the truth that, in the words which Mr. Chesterton has put into Johnson's mouth, "these are they for whom their Omnipotent Creator did not disdain to die"—if, as we have the Fall which forbids us to be proud, we have also the Incarnation which forbids us to despair, then, and then only, is man obviously of final importance in God's scheme. It is a fashion, both among some of those who do and those who do not profess themselves Christians, to speak as if the love of God were an axiom and the Godhead of our Lord an irrelevant addendum to that love, which subsequent investigation might or might not prove to be true. To such talk Johnson never descended.

The argument of the prophet of vanities has, then, very little to do with the miseries of this world.

Emotionally, the temptation to condemn God because of some present sufferings may be almost irresistible. So much of His plan seems to us, so far as we can see it, almost wilfully perverse. Yet only a sentimentalist could mistake such emotionalism for reason and the argument of, say, Hardy's *Dynasts* justifies us neither in condemning Gor nor in patronisingly "ending on a note of hope." Nor is it likely that many can find a lasting refuge in the loud talk of a Henley, "bloody but unbowed," nor in some Swinburnian scepticism, which seeks to comfort man by telling him—what he knows very well to be untrue—that he is "the Master of Things." The complaint that the world is full of sorrow is, as the prophet of vanities knows, no stranger to Christian apologists. The Christian scheme accepts the sorrow of this world; it accounts for it. The prophet asks only whether the account be true or false.

All men have, I suppose, moods in which they are oppressed with a sense of the futility of their lives; they do not feel that they are not fulfilling the purpose for which they were created—that is another and a more valuable mood—but that there is no purpose for them to fulfill. They say with Glycon:

πᾶντα γέλως, καὶ πᾶντα κόνις, καὶ πᾶντα τὸ μήδεν.[1]

This mood Shakespeare used to describe by the metaphor of comparing the world to a stage. The most famous of these comparisons is perhaps more

[1] All is laughter, all is dust, all is nothing.

often quoted than explained but its meaning is, I suppose, that an actor appears to be a free agent, yet really his freedom is a very little thing. He can only repeat the lines which have been written for him and at the end, whether he repeat them right or wrong, whether he play his part well or ill, the piece finishes and the curtain falls, the applause, for what it is worth, very soon dies away, and "the rest is silence." Such, too, is the life of man.

The vague deism of Voltaire or of Burke, the still vaguer deism of Chesterfield, the English gentleman, are not strong enough to conquer this mood. The eighteenth century was an age of many vices; and those vices, as Voltaire rightly insisted and Johnson well knew, were not least evident in the place where they should have been least evident—in the Church. So rank, indeed, had they grown that Christian morals alone were strong enough to stand up against the immorality of Christians. Voltaire had repudiated Christ; *"mais le Christ seul pouvait écraser l'infâme."*

This mood of futility Johnson had felt, had fought and had conquered. If he emerged from his struggles with a hatred of deism, that hatred came, not from mere bigotry, but from the knowledge that, if the Son of God did not become man, then there was no reason to think the human race of serious importance. Life, in Shakespeare's terrible phrase, was a tale, "signifying nothing."

Mr. Belloc, who has written on *Rasselas* and *Candide,* records that it is a pleasure to know that

Johnson was well paid for his work—and so it is. It is a still larger pleasure to know that soon afterwards he was finally freed from financial embarrassments by Lord Bute's offer of a pension of £300 a year—one of the few pensions which that Minister bestowed otherwise than on Scotchmen.

The casuistry of non-juring had always intrigued Johnson—perhaps, because his Jacobite father had taken the oath to the Hanoverian King—and he used to argue with some sense that, if the alternative to taking the oath was to be reduced to such destitution that life could only be supported by crime, then it was better to take it. He asserted that many of the non-juring clergymen, driven by necessity, had gone "to their patrons' wives to bed"—though why such an operation should have been to their financial advantage it is a little hard to see. They would have been better as loyal Hanoverians.

The extreme plea of necessity Johnson could hardly use in his own justification. But the Jacobite cause was now dead, and the old Jacobite justified his acceptance of a Hanoverian pension with a very noble piece of common sense, worthy of the political philosophy of his own Imlac. "I think," he said, "the pleasure of cursing the House of Hanover and drinking King James's health all amply overbalanced by three hundred pounds a year."

A man who is a Jacobite is expected to be romantic. It is a commonplace that English history has been written by Whigs, and the Whig historians have played a very clever trick on their opponents. They have not, as the French have or as the Tudors did with Richard III, vilified them and sent them reeling down to horrified posterity as villains of impossible blackness. More cleverly, they have instead disguised them with a delicate halo of romance. Charles II, the '45, the Southern States in the Civil War—these are problems, we are made to feel, which the scholarly historian should resign to the school of Baroness Orczy, glad to feel that they will receive there the treatment which their attractive absurdities deserve. The best day's work which Macaulay ever did for Whig history was the day on which he wrote *A Jacobite's Epitaph.*

When the Whigs speak of the Continent, they speak of it in a similar language of unreality. They quote Chateaubriand; they keep it dark that there was ever such a man as de Maistre. Yet it was possible to answer Voltaire and the Encyclopædists—and Johnson answered them. There was a perfectly sober, statistical case for Charles II, and Johnson knew it. There were two perfectly sensible sides to a perfectly sensible argument about the '45, and Johnson knew them both. And his true justification for his conduct was less cynical than, though as sane as, the pretended justification.

Parliamentary government necessarily means party government. People divide themselves into sides according to the main issue of the day. We have, for instance, in the twentieth century a Labour party and a capitalist party, and, turn by turn, a

Labour and a capitalist Government. What Parliamentary institutions can never give us is a Government that is impartial between Labour and capital.

Now this impartiality, which is impossible to the Parliamentary politician, is possible to the monarch. For the monarch has no constituents to whom he must justify himself. He need not be a party leader, and this power of impartiality is a great argument for preserving an ancient dynasty on a throne. The argument for restoring a fallen dynasty is clearly very much weaker, for the restored monarch can only scrabble back to the throne as the leader of a party opposed to another party—back into a position, that is to say, in which he is unable to perform the real function of a monarch. The Yorkists under Edward IV, the Stuarts under Charles II and James II, the Bourbons under Louis XVIII and Charles X—all proved that a Restoration, whatever it does, does not restore.

Johnson saw all this. He thought that it was a misfortune that the Stuarts had been turned off, but, misfortune or no, it had happened. Jacobitism was now but a sentimentality, and, even if the Jacobites could be restored to their throne, they could never be restored to their power. The best chance for strong monarchy, small as that chance was, lay in support of George III.

How unreal is the fight of parties, how small is the real difference, how exaggerated the pretended difference between them, none knew better than Johnson. Read the *Idler's* satire on Jacobite and Hanoverian:

"Two of my companions who are grown old in idleness are Tom Tempest and Jack Sneaker. Both of them consider themselves as neglected by their parties and therefore entitled to credit; for why should they favour ingratitude? They are both men of integrity where no factious interest is to be promoted; and both lovers of truth when they are not heated with political debate.

"Tom Tempest is a steady friend to the House of Stuart. He can recount the prodigies that have appeared in the sky and the calamities that have afflicted the nation every year from the Revolution; and is of opinion that, if the exiled family had continued to reign, there would have neither been worms in our ships nor caterpillars in our trees. He wonders that the nation was not awakened by the hard frost to a revocation of the true king and is hourly afraid that the whole island will be lost in the sea. He believes that King William burned Whitehall that he might steal the furniture; and that Tillotson died an atheist. Of Queen Anne he speaks with more tenderness, owns that she meant well and can tell by whom and why she was poisoned. In the succeeding reigns all has been corruption, malice and design. He believes that nothing ill has ever happened for these forty years by chance or errour; he holds that the battle of Dettingen was won by mistake and that of Fontenoy lost by contract; that the Victory was sunk by a private order; that the Cornhill was fired by emissaries from the council; and the arch of Westminster-bridge so contrived as to sink on purpose that the nation might be put to charge. He considers the new road to Islington as an encroachment on liberty and often asserts that broad wheels will be the ruin of England.

"Tom is generally vehement and noisy but nevertheless has some secrets which he always communicates in a whisper. Many and many a time has Tom told me in a corner that our miseries were almost at an end and that we should see in a month another monarch on the throne; the time elapses without a revolution; Tom meets me again with new intelligence, the whole scheme is now settled and we shall see great events in another month.

"Jack Sneaker is a hearty adherent to the present establishment; he has known those who saw the bed into which the Pretender was conveyed in a warming-pan. He often rejoices that the nation was not enslaved by the Irish. He believes that King William never lost a battle and that if he had lived one year longer he would have conquered France. He holds that Charles the First was a Papist. He allows there were some good men in the reign of Queen Anne, but the Peace of Utrecht brought a blast upon the nation and has been the cause of all the evil that we have suffered to the present hour. He believes that the scheme of the South Sea was well intended but that it miscarried by the influence of France. He considers a standing army as the bulwark of liberty, thinks us secured from corruption by septennial Parliaments, relates how we are enriched and strengthened by the electoral dominions and declares that the publick debt is a blessing to the nation."

From the battles of Tweedledum and Tweedledee Johnson had turned to other things. In October of 1765 appeared at last his edition of Shakespeare. "It would be difficult," Macaulay has written, "to name a more slovenly, a more worthless edition of any great classic." The sentence defeats itself by its violence. It is true that, when he first came to Shakespeare, a laudable determination to avoid bardolatry led Johnson into many criticisms that were wilfully outrageous and into an anxiety to refuse to see sense in passages of common quotation where the sense was of the plainest. His note on

> She should have died hereafter;
> There would have been a time for such a word,

where he would have changed "word" to "world," is a good example of this. Yet against this temptation he soon put himself on guard and his final Shakespeare contains much comment but little emendation. "The learning of the ancients," he came to see, "had been long ago obliterated had every man thought himself at liberty to corrupt the lines he did not understand." And in the Preface he wrote with a simplicity engaging, disarming and shattering, "I could have written longer notes, for the art of writing notes is not of difficult attainment."

Macaulay's comment is very silly. Johnson's Shakespeare was certainly not a failure. In a way it was a triumphant success. His book, it is true, contained some strange judgments, such as that there were "no nice discriminations of character in Macbeth." Yet, on the whole, Johnson succeeded all but completely in doing what he tried to do. It is only possible to criticise the performance by criticising the ambition.

In many ways there is a striking similarity between Johnson and Mr. Bernard Shaw. Mr. Shaw men have, it is true, quoted because of his paradoxes, and paradoxes have been necessary in a journalistic age in order to get him a hearing. But he has been believed in because of his platitudes. And, if posterity remembers his name, as I think and hope (for posterity's sake) that it will, it will do so, when *élan vital* and vegetarianism have been long forgotten, or are remembered only as Johnson's orange-peel is remembered, as the splendid incarnation of Philistine John Bullism, the "Great Oddity" of the reign of King Edward VII. In nothing are he and Johnson more similar than in their criticism of Shakespeare.

Both of them have remembered with Aristotle that "it is the function of the critic to criticise," and have rightly refused to surrender themselves to the last absurdity of the romantic, who merely raves where he is asked to judge. Yet it is impossible to criticise save by reference to standard, and the standard by which both Mr. Shaw and Johnson have judged Shakespeare is that of supposing that he was trying to give us a picture of real life. By this standard both of them have been able to tell us a large number of very valuable things. Let us praise them and thank them and read them, but let us at the same time realise that they are judging Shakespeare by standards to which he himself never professed his willingness to submit.

It is but a very little part of Shakespeare's greatness that he "held a mirror up to nature." Realistic art, in the Zolaesque meaning of the words, is almost a contradiction in terms. A man who goes to the theatre in order to get, as Zola told him to get, "a slice out of life," is a fool, for he can clearly get a much better slice, for some *2s.* less, by staying outside. A play of merely imitative realism would be—in fact, is—unbearably boring. It is not necessary to hold any especial brief for the superior Wordsworthian despising the plain, blunt man who is content to call a primrose a primrose. Nevertheless the justification for this art of imitative realism was destroyed once and for all by Alexander the Great, who, when they offered to present to him a man who could sing like a nightingale, answered, "I have heard the nightingale himself."

As Mr. Mencken has said, "The trouble about poetry is that it is a lie"—which, in strict language, it is, for it is an attempt to make words do what of their nature they are incompetent to do. Nobody, meeting Wordsworth wandering, would ever have mistaken him for a cloud. Beaded bubbles do not wink. A nightingale singing never charmed a window—whatever that may mean—and all this Keats very well knew.

The purpose of art is not to teach us lessons upon conduct, but to offer us a refuge from the world of conduct and to strengthen us with the comfort that that world is not all, and Shakespeare, knowing this, cared very little for realism. Shakespeare was very well aware that there never was, nor ever will be, a French physician in the least like Dr. Caius or that young men in Denmark, when they feel like murdering their uncles, do not talk about it in blank verse to themselves and at the tops of their voices. Everybody knows that that Egyptian baggage, Cleopatra, very likely did make jokes about an "old gentleman," as Mr. Shaw would have her do. Everybody knows that she was certainly not capable of, say, that superb piece of rhetoric which begins with the lines:

> Give me my robe; put on my crown.
> I have immortal longings in me.

There is not, I suppose, a plot in Shakespeare which is not so stuffed with absurdities and improbabilities that no modern dramatist would deign to filch it, except perhaps for a purpose of burlesque. What of it?

Who cares for probabilities? Who cares for Cleopatra's nose? Who does not care for Shakespeare's poetry?

If then the whole scheme of a Shakespearean play was deliberately unrealistic, it is absurd to fasten criticism upon this or that detail for its unrealism.

This falseness of standard vitiates Johnson's argument when he agrees with Shakespeare as much as when he disagrees with him. He attacks the unities and defends Shakespeare's indifference to them. Because of this attack, Stendhal reprinted Johnson's Preface bodily in his own *Racine et Shakespeare*—a twisted triumph for classical John Bull. Yet both Johnson and Stendhal—and Dickens, too, who afterwards wrote upon the unities even more absurdly—attacked them without understanding the arguments for them. Johnson says that, even with the unities, no play will ever create the illusion of reality. It is not possible to believe that either Sophocles or Molière were ever such fools as to believe that it would. The argument for the unities has nothing to do with the creation of illusion. It is rather that the mind of the spectator will be more capable of appreciating the beauties of the poetry or the subtleties of the character-drawing if the mere following of the plot does not make a distractingly large demand upon the attention.

Yet, when the great fault in Johnson's Shakespeare has been pointed out and to it have been added doubtless a small list of errors of detail which later patience and ingenuity have been able to discover, you have said all that there is to be said against it. It remains, if not quite, in Adam Smith's phrase, "the most manly piece of criticism that was ever published in any country," at least, to quote Sir Walter Raleigh, "the best bit of eighteenth-century writing on Shakespeare." For, where Johnson erred, he erred with all his century; he excelled them in that he wrote better than they. His book survives triumphantly what must, after all, be the one final test of a book. It is readable.

Of Shakespeare the poet Johnson knew little. Shakespeare the man, the money-grubber, the unconscientious, careless hack-dramatist, he knew through and through, and he was not afraid to tell the truth. "Of all this," he writes at the end of *All's Well That Ends Well,* "Shakespeare could not be ignorant; but Shakespeare wanted to conclude his play."

CHAPTER IV

THE JOHNSONIANS

Literature, if literature means merely the written word, was certainly the loser by King George III's generosity, for Johnson was not, as we have seen, the person to write more than he was forced to write. By nature he was a most social man, a lover of tavern life. "No, sir," he said, "there is nothing which has yet been contrived by man by which so much happiness is produced as by a good tavern, or inn." Conversation was his keenest pleasure, and in conversation he chiefly shone. "Dr. Johnson," reported Fanny Burney, "is indeed very ill favoured; is tall but stoops terribly; he is almost bent double." In repose his face, it is said, was almost imbecile, but, once enlivened by conversation, it became striking and animated.

Little though he thought of the cant which would be for ever singing the praises of poverty, he was himself one of those who always preferred a moderate income and leisure to wealth won only at the price of continual labour. "Getting money is not all a man's business." Three hundred pounds a year, even when the large claims of his charity and his seraglio have been allowed for, were almost sufficient for his needs, and for the rest of his life it is for the most part (though not exclusively) Johnson the talker whom we meet—that Johnson whom we know best—that Johnson whom we love most—that Johnson who best deserves both to be known and to be loved.

To the historian his gigantic figure has come so wholly to dominate the social life of the latter half of the eighteenth century that we are almost apt to forget that there was any circle of which he was not a member. If a dramatist were to write an historical play upon the period, it would be considered almost an eccentricity if he did not make Dr. Johnson one of his characters. Yet not only was there a society—of which the Memoirs of Horace Walpole, for instance, give us a picture—into which Johnson was never admitted, but that society which excluded Johnson, rightly or wrongly, considered itself the best society. The reason for its exclusiveness is easy to understand and very fairly easy to pardon. Johnson was excluded because of what I should like to call his love of equality, because of what those less favourable to him would perhaps call (and sometimes, I am afraid, with justice) his bad manners. Chesterfield's comment on Johnson was that "this absurd person was not only uncouth in manners and warm in dispute but behaved exactly in the same way to superiors, equals and inferiors, and therefore by a necessary consequence absurdly to two of the three." Johnson's own account of it was that "great lords and great ladies don't love to have their mouths stopped."

Johnson had, too, a voracity for every kind of life which made him intolerable to anyone whose own nature was at all snobbish or finicky. "Dr. Johnson's knowledge and esteem of what we call low or coarse life was prodigious," says Mrs. Thrale; and, though Johnson denied it, Mrs. Thrale was certainly right. He had known, he boasted, all the wits, "from Mrs. Montague to Bet Flint," and, when asked who Bet Flint might be, explained, "Oh, a fine character, madam; she was habitually a slut and a drunkard and occasionally a thief and a harlot." He announced that he would even have accompanied Boswell to see Mrs. Rudd, a woman of somewhat easy virtue who had saved her life by turning King's evidence on her paramour, were it not that "now they have a trick of putting everything into the newspapers."

It is impossible to pretend that Johnson's bad manners can always be fairly excused as merely a too rugged search after truth. He had contracted—whether, as Macaulay suggests, in Grub Street or elsewhere—habits which were by no means good for a lady's crockery or upholstery, to say nothing of the offence to an æsthetic sense. Most ladies, I suppose, are inclined to sympathise with the complaints of Mrs. Boswell and to wonder concerning Mrs. Thrale, not why she turned against Johnson at last, but how she was able to tolerate him for so long.

"Who's for poonsh?" Garrick describes Johnson as saying, as he squeezed a lemon through very dirty fingers into a punch-bowl, and adds, "He must have been a stout man who would have been for it." Of the taking of baths Johnson said, "Let well alone and be content. I hate immersion." There is an often-repeated story, of which I cannot trace the source, that a lady with whom he was riding in a coach once found it necessary to complain that he smelt. "Nay, madam," answered Johnson, the enemy, as ever, of the sloppy phrase, "give me leave to correct you. You smell; I stink."

"I have seen many a bear led by a man," said Mrs. Boswell of her husband and his friend, "but I never before saw a man led by a bear"; and she objected to his turning the candles head downwards and letting the wax fall on the carpet. The objection is intelligible. His habit also of always "pulling a little book out" when he was not entertained by whatever conversation might be going on was, as Mrs. Thrale says, "more likely to advance the growth of science than of polished manners."

There was a rugged honesty about Johnson which caused him to take an invitation in the strictest sense. When he was asked out to dine, he went to dine, not to fulfil a social engagement. "I mind my belly very studiously and very carefully," he said, "for I look upon it that he who does not mind his belly will hardly mind anything else." And everybody is familiar with the peculiar way in which he set about the minding of his belly.

"I never knew any man," writes the very veracious Boswell, "who relished good eating as he did. When at table he was totally absorbed in the business of the moment; his looks seemed riveted to his plate; nor would he, unless when in very high company, say one word, or even pay the least attention, till he had satisfied his appetite which was so fierce and indulged with such intenseness that while in the act of eating the veins of his forehead swelled and generally a strong perspiration was visible."

"Βρῶσις ὀλίγη"[1] is the laconic and disgusted entry in his diary after a day of short commons at the house of a friend of Mrs. Thrale. He complained of the Parisian and the Scotch footmen who used their fingers as sugar-tongs. The peccadillo was very mild in comparison with many of his own so that, if one considers the table-manners that he was willing to permit himself, it is most surprising to learn from Miss Reynolds that he "had a great dislike to the use of a pocket-handkerchief at meals, when, if he happened to have occasion for one, he would rise from his chair and go to some distance with his back to the company and perform the operation as silently as possible."

One had again to be prepared for occasional fits of absolutely unreasonable peevishness. When, for instance, Boswell had at some trouble arranged for Lord Marchmont to call on Johnson to give him some

[1] "Little to eat."

details of Pope's life for the *Lives of the Poets,* Johnson, for no reason at all, utterly refused to meet him. There are other instances of such behaviour.

There was then a price to be paid for the pleasures of Johnson's conversation; and in the conversation itself a competitiveness that was not wholly pleasant. He talked for victory, as undergraduates do. But when one has said these two things one has said all that there is to be said against Johnson as a conversationalist. If one was to say all that there was to be said for him there would be no stopping.

Reynolds claimed that "he qualified my mind to think justly. No man had like him the faculty of teaching inferior minds the art of thinking." Johnson's peculiar excellence lay in his power of just distinguishing. It was often possible to predict his opinions; it was never possible to predict the argument with which he would defend those opinions. His distinctions were hardly ever original, but they were always lucid and always important.

One can open Boswell at random for illustrations of this. Take the sentence: "Sir, I have found you an argument. I am not obliged to find you an understanding." Or read the letter which he wrote to Boswell on the latter's unfortunate differences with his father, in which the distinction is drawn between "the kindness of a parent, which can always be commanded," and "the fondness which is not within our power."

The man who talked with Johnson was forced continually to think and to say what he meant. That sloppy blurring of distinctions into which conversation is apt to collapse was impossible in his presence. He gave, to use his own phrase, "confidence to truth." Where the truth had before seemed weak and sentimental and ridiculous, he showed it to be rational and strong. He turned the laugh against the lie. And to do that is to be a very great servant of truth.

Johnson was the greatest of all English talkers. And talk in the eighteenth century was not the hurried, half-shameful, modern thing in which we indulge with an apology for the hour that is snatched from business. Johnson himself but once in his life, he said, refused an invitation to dinner because he had work to do, and then he regretted it and did no work. Few sights in the world are more contemptible than that of a man unnecessarily in a hurry, feverishly rushing he knows not whence and he knows not whither, and there is a petty punctuality which is most damnably the thief of time. Wesley was the only forerunner of the modern busy man into whose company Johnson ever came, and Johnson did not like him any the better for it.

> "John Wesley's conversation," he said, "is good, but he is never at leisure. He is always obliged to go at a certain hour. This is very disagreeable to a man who loves to fold his legs and have out his talk as I do."

Conversation came to be by far the largest pleasure of his life, as indeed it is that of most good men—at least, of most of those good men who lack the refuge of a family. "The visits of idle, and some of them very worthless, persons," complains Sir John Hawkins, "were never unwelcome to him, and, though they interrupted him in his studies and meditations, yet as they gave him opportunities of discourse and furnished him with intelligence he strove rather to protract than to shorten or discountenance them."

It takes two to make a conversation, as it takes two to make a quarrel. And were I to write of all the people with whom Johnson conversed I might write for ever. One must select. There are some who are only interesting because Johnson did converse with them. Of this class was Taylor, Johnson's old schoolfellow, the Rector of Market Bosworth and "the King of Ashbourne." The two differed on most things. They differed on politics; they differed on emetics. Taylor thought that he would break some vessels if he took an emetic. "Bah!" said Johnson, who "did not know a character more disagreeable than a valetudinarian," "if you have so many things that will break you had better break your neck at once and there's an end on't." Taylor was a Whig, a strong Hanoverian, and so little did the pair seem to have in common that Boswell, with less than his usual charity, suggests that Johnson was after his school-friend's money. If such were his designs they were frustrated, for Taylor survived him, and, as a Prebendary of Westminster, lived to read the funeral service over his old friend with, as was thought, a disgustingly small display of emotion. Of him Johnson explained, with a perhaps unnecessary precision, "Sir, I love him but I do not love him more; my regard for him does not increase."

A more interesting man was David Garrick. He was, as has been said, one of the few pupils whom Johnson in his schoolmastering days had succeeded in attracting to his strange academy. Johnson and Garrick had come up to London together to make their fortune. Nor can it be denied that Johnson was never quite able to free himself from jealousy that the pupil should have succeeded in making it much more quickly than the master. He seems, too, to have thought that Garrick was partly responsible for the failure of *Irene*—in which he certainly did him an injustice. To be continually outstripped by his pupils is one of a schoolmaster's necessary crosses, and those who remember—as everyone does remember—the story of that first, famous meeting between Boswell and his master in Tom Davies's parlour will know that Johnson would never allow another to speak any evil of David Garrick. Yet it was only that the monopoly might be reserved to himself.

Garrick was very well aware of the opinion which was held of him and he used to mimic Johnson's sneers. "Davy has some convivial pleasantry about him," he would make Johnson say, "but 'tis a futile fellow."

There are some stories of Johnson's behaviour to Garrick which do not make wholly pleasant reading. In the end, it is true, he supported Garrick for the club, and, when Garrick died, even insisted that the club should go into a year's widowhood. Yet there is something very offensive in his first opposition to Garrick's membership. Nor was the revenge which he took for Garrick's very natural reluctance to lend him his copy of old plays at all a worthy one. Johnson was not, as he should himself have known, so tender in his treatment of books that even his oldest friends could be reasonably expected to lend him a work of value.

It is the fashion to ascribe to mere prejudice Johnson's contempt for actors. That fashion is, I think, not fair. The actor who consents to spend his existence in repeating another man's comments on life has no right to pretend that his is an art similar to that of the poet or the musician. It is not necessary to defend any Puritanical hatred of the stage. That people should amuse themselves by seeing plays is very legitimate. For plays provide, to use Johnsonese, "a stock of harmless pleasures"—and there can hardly be plays if there are not also players. Players should receive a salary for what they do, and there are among them better actors and worse, "as some dogs dance better than others." But everybody must have discovered among his own acquaintances, as Johnson discovered, that, when an actor ceases to be somebody else and has for a few moments to become himself, it is often surprising how very empty a man he is. The great tragic actor is, as often as not, inarticulate for a single sentence.

Garrick, if we are to accept George Colman's word for it, was no exception to this rule. When "he chose to show off as himself . . . he was almost sure to play that character worse than any other."

Johnson has, in his note on Bottom, left us an opinion on actors which is quite untinged by personality. "Bottom discovers a true genius for the stage by his solicitude for propriety of dress and his deliberation which beard to choose among many beards, all unnatural." A play, he said, that is worth very much is often "the worse for being acted." "*Macbeth*, for instance," and, I would add, almost all great plays. A great writer has the power to tell us what he has to tell us directly. An actor or a theatre between us and him is an obstruction. The actor misinterprets, or interprets where the writer had left us to think out for ourselves what should be the interpretation. Some men, it may be, cannot believe in King Lear until they see him on the stage. Others cannot believe that he is a King until they see him wearing a crown. But to the actor who panders to this smallness of imagination we do not owe gratitude.

It is very easy to understand then Johnson's annoyance at the extravagant reputation which Garrick gained. Yet it is not a pleasant trait which, when it can find nothing else to grumble at, grumbles at the ill-deserved good fortune of one's oldest friend. Yet there are pleasanter pictures of their relations. In a letter of Hannah More's, for instance, we find:

> "Garrick was the very soul of the company, and I never saw Johnson in such perfect good humour. We have often heard that one can never properly enjoy the company of these two unless they are together. There is great truth in this remark; for after the Dean and Mrs. Boscawen (who were the only strangers) were gone, Johnson and Garrick began a close encounter, telling old stories 'e'en from their boyish days' at Lichfield. We all stood round them above an hour laughing."

When Garrick died, Johnson said, as is known, that his death had "eclipsed the gaiety of nations." Cumberland records that at his funeral "I saw old Samuel Johnson standing beside his grave at the foot of Shakespeare's monument, and bathed in tears." Yet it is hard to blame Mrs. Garrick, who did not respond to the suggestion that her husband's life should be written by his old tutor.

Another peculiar acquaintance of Johnson was the little lawyer, Edwards, who had been with Johnson at Pembroke, and who met him again in the street after an interval of fifty years. Johnson, in flattery and pretended envy, spoke of Edwards as a man of the world and of himself as a poor bookworm. Yet it is clear that Edwards was really a dull and very narrow fool and that Johnson knew many times more about the world than he did. Nor would he be remembered at all were it not for one very good thing which he somehow happened to say. "You are a philosopher, Dr. Johnson," he remarked one day. "I have tried, too, in my time to be a philosopher; but, I don't know how, cheerfulness was always breaking in." It was very likely the one good remark of a lifetime and it has lived for 150 years by the curious chance that it was made to Johnson.

Then there was Bathurst, the doctor, whom Johnson liked because he was "a good hater," and who died at Havannah and left Johnson his negro-servant, Frank. After Bathurst's death, Johnson used often to mention him in his prayers. There was Hawkesworth, too, who wrote—or at any rate sold, for it seems uncertain how much of the writing was his own—an account of some voyages to the South Seas in which was a sceptical speculation upon the possibility of miracles. His scepticism was bitterly attacked and the not so very fiery particle was snuffed out by the article. He died soon afterwards, his death, according to Malone, being caused by an overdose of opium.

After these came the two friends, Bennet Langton and Topham Beauclerk—Langton, whom Boswell did not like but of whom Johnson said, "The earth does not bear a worthier man than Bennet Langton"; Beauclerk, the descendant of Charles II, in Johnson's opinion the last King of England. Johnson liked his friend the better for his descent from the monarch and the monarch the better for his ancestry of the friend. Beauclerk had inherited more than royal blood from his royal ancestor. He had inherited also that quality which caused royal blood to flow in so very many and various veins among all classes of the country. Yet for some reason Johnson was not here inclined to play the stern moralist and was willing to overlook these vagaries in Topham Beauclerk. He said of Beauclerk's wife, "The woman's a whore and there's an end on't." But he had, as it seems, no objection to her being also from time to time a hostess. "Sir, I would walk to the extent of the diameter of the earth to save Beauclerk," said Johnson of him in his last illness; and, when he died, wrote to Boswell:

> "Poor, dear Beauclerk—*nec, ut soles, dabis ioca.* His wit and his folly, his acuteness and maliciousness, his merriment and reasoning are now over. Such another will not often be found among mankind."

Everybody knows the story of how Langton and Beauclerk one night, having sat up at a tavern until three in the morning, determined that they would go and knock old Johnson up. Johnson came to the door, poker in hand and with an old wig on his head for a nightcap. But discovering, not a burglar, but his two friends, he exclaimed, "What is it, you dogs? I'll have a frisk with you." And the three spent the rest of the night together, first in a Covent Garden tavern, later in the dignified and philosophic amusement of going in a boat to Billingsgate.

Against Langton Johnson seems to have had but two objections—that he could not manage his money and that "he has his children too much about him." Johnson, though fond of children, could not bear to hear them perform before grown-ups. When an affectionate father once suggested that his children should recite in turn Gray's *Elegy,* and that he should then judge which had done it the better, he said, "No, pray, sir, let the dears both speak it at once; more noise will by that means be made and the noise will be sooner over." Of Langton's children he similarly complained. "The father is never easy when he is not making them do something which they cannot do; they must repeat a fable or a speech or the Hebrew alphabet; and they might as well count twenty for what they know of the matter; however, the father says half, for he prompts every other word." And Mrs. Thrale agreed with him that "nothing is more ridiculous than parents cramming their children's nonsense down other people's throats."

It was while he was a guest at Langton's house that Johnson insisted on rolling down a hill, excusing himself by saying that he "had not had a roll for some time." So he lay himself down at the top of the hill,

Portrait of Johnson

from a painting by Barry

and over and over he went until at last he came to the bottom. It is a most extraordinary story. The date was 1766. Johnson was at that time fifty-seven. The dictionary was out almost ten years. The Shakespeare was to appear in the next year. He was the first living figure of English letters. There is no one to-day with whom one can compare him in order to convince the reader's imagination of the oddity of Johnson's behaviour. The Poet Laureate or Sir Edmund Gosse, Mr. George Moore or a Regius Professor—none of them, I suspect, have "had a roll for some time."

In a third and perhaps yet stranger scene of Johnson's life Bennet Langton played his part. On May 10th, 1773, Boswell and Johnson went to dine with General Paoli. But Johnson was ill, and had to leave the table. He appointed Boswell to meet him later in the evening at "Mr. (now Sir Robert) Chambers's in the Temple." When Boswell arrived there he found Johnson in no good temper. Chambers was officiously suggesting remedies for his health, and Johnson angrily answering, "Prythee don't teeze me. Stay till I am well, and then you shall tell me how to cure myself."

As time passed "he grew better." Conversation turned on Bennet Langton's will which Chambers happened to have made that very day. Langton had left his estate to his three sisters. Of this Johnson greatly disapproved, calling them "three dowdies," and was, it seems, proceeding to lay about him in his best bludgeoning style. Suddenly, incomprehensibly, his mood changed. For a reason which Chambers could not guess, which Boswell could not guess, which we cannot guess to-day, it struck him as irresistibly comic that Bennet Langton should make a will.

> "He now laughed immoderately without any reason that we could perceive at our friend's making his will; calling him the testator and adding, 'I daresay he thinks he has done a mighty thing. He won't stay till he gets home to his seat in the country to produce this wonderful deed: he'll call up the landlord of the first inn on the road; and after a suitable preface upon mortality and the uncertainty of life will tell him that he should not delay making his will; and here, sir, will he say, is my will which I have just made with the assistance of one of the ablest lawyers in the kingdom; and he will read it to him (laughing all the time). He believes he has made this will; but he did not make it: you, Chambers, made it for him. I trust you have had more conscience than to make him say "being of sound understanding"; ha, ha, ha, I hope he has left me a legacy. I'd have his will turned into verse like a ballad.'
>
> "In this playful manner did he run on."

Chambers, the self-important lawyer, was not amused. "Mr. Chambers did not by any means relish this jocularity upon a matter of which *pars magna fuit* and seemed impatient till he got rid of us." Yet it needed more than a turning-out-of-doors to stop Johnson's laughter on this Gargantuan night.

> "Johnson could not stop his merriment, but continued it all the way until he got without the Temple-gate. He then burst into such a fit of laughter that he appeared to be almost in a convulsion; and, in order to support himself, laid hold of one of the posts at the side of the foot pavement and sent forth peals so loud that in the silence of the night his voice seemed to resound from Temple Bar to Fleet Ditch."

As Mr. Beerbohm says, "Echoes of that huge laughter come ringing down the ages."

> What were seen? None knows, none ever shall know.

Boswell, the consummate artist, recognised that he was here in the presence of some business of which he could never hope to know the meaning. "Not such as might be expected of the author of the *Rambler*" is the impeccable schoolma'am's comment on Johnson's conduct. Yet he did not interrupt with, "Pray, sir, what is there amusing in Bennet Langton making a will?" or "Is it not better, sir, that a man should make a will rather than leave his dependants to quarrel over his estate?" Nor did he try to dam the torrent by some maddening irrelevance such as, "Sir, what would you do if a gentleman were to ask your advice on sailcloth?"

What did he do? He let Johnson have his laugh

out—there was no stopping him—and then, when at last that gigantic shapelessness that was Samuel Johnson had been shaken almost to pulp, the amazing end of this amazing story comes on us so suddenly and so quietly as almost to take our breath away. "I accompanied him to his door," writes Boswell, "where he gave me his blessing."

What an extraordinary tale! It takes less than half a page in Boswell. Has there been since his day any other writer of English, except perhaps Dickens, who could make such a scene live so vividly before us?

I have no idea what Johnson was laughing at. I refuse to speculate. Browning, you will remember, tells us how among artists there is

> None but would forego his proper dowry,
>
> . . . .
>
> Put to proof art alien to the artist's,
> Once and only once.

May it not be so, too, with the humourist? His life was lived out among the laughter of many men. The world was intolerably about him. God gave to him no mystic, solitary vision. Yet he, too, had his hour that night at Temple Bar. Old Chambers had barred his door and gone disgustedly to bed. Boswell was there, but only there as a witness and a recorder. The world for once was absent, when there roared out under the stars, and "from Temple Bar to Fleet Ditch," that enormous laughter at the joke of Bennet

Langton's will which Samuel Johnson shared alone with God.

Yet I confess that I would like to know more of this Bennet Langton. He seems to have been a good man, a little like a crane, a kind father, a poor business man, a bibliophile, a very respectable citizen, so that people wondered that he went about so much with Topham Beauclerk. Why did Johnson roll down a hill when he happened to be Langton's guest? Why did he upset barrows in Covent Garden in Langton's company? Why did he laugh to the stars? Why did he choose Langton, out of all his friends, to tell him his faults? Why did he say that Langton, out of all his friends, would most certainly go to heaven?

A better-known friend of Johnson was Sir Joshua Reynolds, one of the greatest of all portrait-painters and a writer of more than respectable talent. Whatever it was that attracted Johnson to Reynolds it was not his art, for Johnson had neither the æsthetic nor the physical capacity to appreciate a picture. He was too blind to see it and too inartistic to have known whether it was good or bad even had he been able to see it. Reynolds, like all Johnson's friends, was very considerably his junior, and it is at first a little difficult to see what they did have in common. Yet there was in Reynolds's conversation a certain wisdom of the world, an absence of cant, very similar to Johnson's own, and which, in a canting world, Johnson found very attractive.

Their first meeting was in 1752 at the house of Miss Cotterell. The ladies there were lamenting the loss of a friend and benefactor. "You have, however," said Reynolds, "the comfort of being relieved from a burden of gratitude."

It was the sort of thing which everyone knows to be true, but which very few venture to say, the sort of thing which Johnson always loved to say and loved to hear others saying. Johnson and Reynolds were friends for life.

It was a remark in the same class as Johnson's reply to Boswell's question as to what he "would do if he heard that one of his intimate friends was in danger of being hanged."

"I should do what I could to bail him and give him any other assistance; but if he were once fairly hanged I should not suffer."

"Would you eat your dinner that day, sir?"

"Yes, sir," came the answer, "and eat it as if he were eating with me."

The modern world has come to value kindness above truth. To us therefore both remarks may seem somewhat brutal. On a pagan philosophy such a preference is reasonable. Yet Johnson and Reynolds shared neither the philosophy nor the preference. To them therefore the obligation of truth was paramount and "truth," as Newman truly said, "is aggressive."

Joshua Reynolds was in some ways the most attractive of all Johnson's friends. It would be very easy to write a life of him and, doing so, to convince the reader of the wise and noble, gentle and generous soul that he was; it is very hard to give a picture of him in a few paragraphs. For he had no clear-cut opinions which can be summarised in a sentence or two, as had Goldsmith or Burke. He had no vices, like Beauclerk or Wilkes; no eccentricities, like Boswell. Odd things did not happen in his company as they happened in that of Bennet Langton. His life was quiet and of a piece. As Austin Dobson has written in his *Gentleman of the Old School:*

> Doubtless you
> With too serene a conscience drew
> Your easy breath and slumbered through
> The gravest issue;
> But we to whom our age allows
> Scarce space to wipe our weary brows

cannot but envy the former age which produced a Joshua Reynolds. There is at least one enormous proof that although a man of peace yet he was not therefore a man without character. He was the only person at whose rebuke Johnson was ever certainly observed to blush.

A man more distinguished even than Reynolds was Edmund Burke, the first of English orators, as it seems to be admitted by generations which have not had the opportunity of listening to his speeches. Of all his remarkable friends Johnson never made it a secret that he considered Burke to be by far the most remarkable.

> "If a man went under a shed at the same time with Burke to avoid a shower he would say, 'This is an extraordinary man.' Or if Burke went into a stable to see his horse dressed the ostler would say, 'We have had an extraordinary man here.' "

When Johnson was lying ill he said that, were Burke to come into the room at that moment, it would kill him, so great was his friend's power of intellectual stimulation. Burke on the other hand said of Johnson, "It is enough for me to have rung the bell for him."

This great admiration which the two friends had for one another may seem surprising to one who thinks of their difference in their political opinions. It is the more surprising when we remember that the period of their friendship was also that of the American quarrel. Yet to Johnson private things were always more important than public things. "To be happy at home is the ultimate result of all ambition." Even of Fox he said, "I am for the King against Fox; but I am for Fox against Pitt"; and explained that the reason was that "the King is my master; but I do not know Pitt: and Fox is my friend." Fox was a far more outrageous Whig and a far less intimate friend than Burke. Indeed, Fox hardly ever dared to open his mouth in Johnson's company. Johnson was willing, therefore, to pardon in Burke political opinions which he was unwilling to pardon in others.

To Johnson, Burke was "a bottomless Whig." He

meant by that, I suppose, that his Whiggery was a mere invitation to disruption; that, though Burke professed a belief in an aristocracy, yet the logical conclusion of his arguments was not aristocracy but anarchy. The demand of Johnson's Toryism was that each person should accept the organisation of society in which he found himself and his own place in that organisation. Johnson preferred an organisation in which political responsibility was in the hands of one man, but he could understand a Venetian constitution in which it was in the hands of a gang. He even came to have an affection and admiration for such a man as Sir Robert Walpole, who could accept oligarchy with as little illusion concerning the virtues of oligarchs as had Johnson concerning the virtues of monarchs when he accepted monarchy. For there are very few to whom the world owes more than it does to those who save it from an irrelevant controversy. That under any form of government power will often be in the hands of bad men seemed to him obvious, and he liked to argue with those who saw this as clearly as did he.

If a man were to tell him that he would substitute for the divine right of Stuarts a divine right of Cavendishes, Russels and Pelhams, Johnson, while not agreeing that the substitution was an improvement, could at any rate understand. The merely negative invitation of *une carrière ouverte aux talents*—the invitation to people not to accept their position in life, to scramble, without even an agreed umpire who should decide which talents should be rewarded with which posts—he could not understand. That was to him "bottomless Whiggery."

Whether or not it was just to charge Burke with it is another question. It was to be the complaint of the great Tory of the nineteenth century that the Whigs formed a Venetian oligarchy; it was the complaint of the great Tory of the eighteenth century that they did nothing of the sort. Neither, it is safe to say, was wholly right. For neither fully appreciated the great wisdom of the Whigs—that almost uncanny instinct which the English alone among oligarchies seem to have possessed—the instinct that when there is something really important to be done you must get someone who is not a gentleman to do it. The Whigs shot Byng; they sent Cumberland to capitulate at Klosterseven. Such were the occupations of gentlemen in time of war. But it was Clive and Wolfe, Rodney and Nelson, whom they harnessed to save England and oligarchy in their peril. Yet the spirit which thus used the middle classes was very different from that equalitarian revolution.

Yet had Johnson lived only a few years longer, he would have seen that spirit. It would have been for him a melancholy old age, yet he would have been able to find for himself at least one consolation. While everything else that he loved was either going down into destruction or at the least in deadly peril, he might have comforted himself with the thought that the cataclysm which had turned all the rest of the world into a madhouse had at the least turned Burke into a Tory.

Macaulay has raised the question why, if Johnson thought that political arrangements made so small a difference to human happiness and that under any constitution they would be made by selfish men for selfish motives, why, if he "would not give half a guinea to live under one form of government rather than another," did he then bother to be a Tory rather than a Whig? If his philosophy is correct, "it is not easy," says Macaulay, "to see how Whiggism can be viler than Toryism, or how the Crown can have too little power."

The answer to this difficulty has been given by Leslie Stephen. According to Johnson, political and social arrangements had to be made. *How* they were made mattered very little: still less did it matter who made them. But *that* they were made did matter. Johnson said that he would not give half a guinea to live under one form of government rather than another. He never said that he would not give half a guinea to avoid living under no form of government at all. It was his argument, as it was to be afterwards that of de Maistre, that Whig philosophy gave no motive from which a citizen should obey the sovereign if he did not want to, and that its logical conclusion, whether the individual saw it or not, was anarchy. To the Tory, grievances exist and are to be remedied; to the Whig, if they do not exist, they are to be created.

Take Johnson's account of the raising of a petition against the Government.

"The progress of a petition is well known. An ejected placeman goes down to his county or his borough, tells his friends of his inability to serve them and his constituents of the corruption of the Government. His friends readily understand that he who can get nothing will have nothing to give. They agree to proclaim a meeting. Meat and drink are plentifully provided, a crowd is easily brought together and those who think that they know the reason of the meeting undertake to tell those who know it not. Ale and clamour unite their powers; the crowd, condensed and heated, begins to ferment with the leaven of sedition. All see a thousand evils though they cannot show them and grow impatient for a remedy though they know not what.

"A speech is then made by the Cicero of the day; he says much and suppresses more and credit is equally given to what he tells and what he conceals. The petition is heard and universally approved. Those who are sober enough to write add their names, and the rest would sign if they could.

"Every man goes home and tells his neighbour of the glories of the day, how he was consulted and what he advised; how he was invited into the great room where his lordship caressed him by his name; how he was caressed by Sir Francis, Sir Joseph and

Sir George; how he ate turtle and venison and drank unanimity to the brothers.

"The poor loiterer whose shop had confined him or whose wife had locked him up hears the tale of luxury with envy and at last inquires what was their petition. Of the petition nothing is remembered by the narrator, but that it spoke much of fears and apprehensions and something very alarming, but that he is sure it is against the Government.

"The other is convinced that it must be right and wishes he had been there, for he loves wine and venison and resolves as long as he lives to be against the Government.

"The petition is then handed from town to town and from house to house, and wherever it comes the inhabitants flock together that they may see that which must be sent to the King. Names are easily collected. One man signs because he hates the papists; another because he has vowed destruction to the turnpikes; one because it will vex the parson; another because he owes his landlord nothing; one because he is rich; another because he is poor; one to show that he is not afraid; and another to show that he can write."

Doubtless this is a one-sided picture. Still it is important to recognise that it is one side of the picture. Only the other day some hundreds of Californian girl students signed a piece of paper demanding that they themselves should be immediately executed simply because it was presented to them in the form of a petition. The mechanism is doubtless often of honest use for the ventilation of the grievance. As often, or almost as often, the mechanism creates the grievance. An opposition must either oppose or die. The voter at an election, like the man before the shop window, "is tempted to contrive wants for the pleasure of supplying them."

Only less remarkable, if less remarkable, than Burke was Johnson's other Irish friend, Oliver Goldsmith. As conversationalists there was no comparison between the two. Burke was generally agreed to be, after Johnson, the greatest talker of his time. Goldsmith "talked like poor Poll." An absurd eagerness to shine was always causing him to talk when he had nothing to say or when he had not given himself time to think out what it was that he was going to say. An absurd sensitiveness to ridicule was always causing him to make himself ridiculous, while, even if he did not make himself ridiculous, nature had stamped him with features so ugly as to be themselves sufficient to create any normal amount of ridicule.

> A queer little fellow, grave-featured, pock-pitten,
> Though they say in his cups he's as gay as a kitten,

is Austin Dobson's description of him.

The truth was, I suppose, that Goldsmith was conscious, as he could not very well help being conscious, that his powers were superior to those of other men.

Yet these superior powers were by no means combined with a superiority to petty vanity. At the same time he lacked social advantages and social graces. Therefore he was continually tormented with misery when, in a company, he saw another cutting a larger figure than himself. As may be guessed, a man with such a character had often, in the company of Johnson, to find himself miserable.

At times too, it must be admitted, Goldsmith's vexation was intelligible. The two supped one night with an Eton master called Graham. Looking at Goldsmith, Graham said, "Doctor, I shall be glad to see you at Eton."

"I shall be glad to wait on you," said Goldsmith.

"No, 'tis not you, I mean, Doctor Minor," said Graham. " 'Tis Doctor Major there!!"

Goldsmith said, "Graham is a fellow to make one commit suicide," and even those of us who most pride ourselves on our superiority to petty vanity might have found it difficult to be quite unruffled at such treatment.

Goldsmith's talent, while less overwhelming, was far more delicate than that of Johnson. One might have expected Johnson to have been indifferent to it and to have jeered away his work as finicky cant. But this he never did. From the first he always understood that in Goldsmith he had a friend of genius, and he even seems to have taken some pains in society to pander to Goldsmith's susceptibilities and to try, when he could remember to do so, to restrain the too heavy bludgeonings of his own wit. Yet, as can well be imagined, the excitement of talk was often too much. Often, too, Goldsmith was frankly impossible. As Boswell suggests, Goldsmith had not perhaps more envy than other people, but he at least spoke of it more. He was also a liar—though a liar of an engagingly simple type who hardly tried to deceive. Take, for instance, his story, which all knew to be false, that his brother was the Dean of Durham. Yet Johnson demanded an almost inhuman standard of casual accuracy. Between the two, then, quarrels were frequent. But Johnson was always anxious to make things up as soon as might be. "Doctor Goldsmith, Doctor Goldsmith," he would cry, "we had some words to-day. I ask your pardon"; and all was well.

Everyone knows the story of how the two friends one day found themselves together in the Poets' Corner of Westminster Abbey. Johnson turned to Goldsmith.

> Forsitan et nostrum nomen miscebitur istis,

he quoted. They passed a little later by Temple Bar, still crowned by the heads of those executed after that last Jacobite rising with which both had a lingering sympathy.

> Forsitan et nostrum nomen miscebitur istis,

quoted Goldsmith, pointing to the heads. Both prophecies have been proved true.

Goldsmith was as incapable of business as he was of social behaviour. One day in 1764 his landlady had him arrested for debt. He appealed to Johnson, and Johnson at once sent him a guinea and soon after followed himself to see what could be done. On his arrival he found Goldsmith in bed and by his bedside a bottle of Madeira, for the purchase of which he had spent a part of Johnson's guinea and with which he was consoling himself. Johnson corked the bottle and asked Goldsmith if he had any asset which could be of use for the defraying of the debt. Goldsmith's only property was a manuscript. This he gave to Johnson and Johnson, going out, sold it to a bookseller and returned with £60. The name of the manuscript was *The Vicar of Wakefield.*

Few can read *The Vicar of Wakefield* without delight in its vivid, quaint and delicate picture of middle-class life. Yet I think that the critic errs who estimates Goldsmith's place in the world of letters chiefly by it. *The Traveller* and *The Deserted Village* are far deeper works. Goldsmith deserves the prophet's praise. He challenged industrialism before industrialism was fairly begun. While the parliamentarian was still talking of himself as a liberator, Goldsmith was already talking of him as an oppressor and bidding us "fly from petty tyrants to the throne." Many of those doubts and denunciations which were afterwards to make the stuff of Cobbett's great rhetoric first appear in English literature in the delicate verse of Oliver Goldsmith.

How just were these doubts this is not the place to discuss. The charge is often made against Goldsmith that Johnson did not think him particularly clear-headed. One can only answer in the language of the just rebuke given to the young man who claimed that Johnson had himself confessed to not being a good Greek scholar. "Sir, it is not easy to say what such a man as Dr. Johnson would call a good Greek scholar." Still less is it easy to say what such a man as Dr. Johnson would call a clear head.

Doubtless some of Goldsmith's ideas were fantastic, some tinged with cant. His almost incredible ignorance of facts—consider, for instance, the ease with which Gibbon was able to persuade him that Alexander the Great was the conqueror of Montezuma—betrayed him into absurdity as soon as he started to speak of anything not within his own experience. Yet in his delicacy of mind and his power to understand forms of life different from his own—that, for instance, of the Italian or of the countryman—Goldsmith was certainly Johnson's superior. "He had," complains Sir John Hawkins, "no sense of the shame nor dread of the evils of poverty." That is to say, he loved the poor and refused to compete. And, with all his deficiencies, he stands, on the whole, second, I suppose, only to Johnson among the literary Tories of the eighteenth century. That is high praise, for they were a very noble crowd indeed.

These Tories really tried to tell the truth, to speak of man as he was, and this is a much rarer thing than most of us like to admit. It is—or at least has been since the French Revolution—a continual temptation to pretend that by some small change of machinery all human unhappiness can be abolished. We must eat Empire butter, or read Miss ——'s poems, or nationalise the mines, or inhibit our metabolisms, or study the works of a Serbian gentleman who draws navels to look like soup-plates, or indulge whatever may be the appropriate fad, and all will be well.

There is a wise, balanced, comprehensive philosophy which would allow to each of these activities its appropriate importance. Subjected to such a philosophy, they would each be useful. Without it they are at the worst dangerous, at the best futile. For all such promises men know in their heart of hearts to be lies. They play with them to save themselves from despair. And it is wiser to tell the truth with Johnson and Goldsmith. The machinery and habits of life have their importance and it is sane to take a little trouble to improve them. Yet in the end human unhappiness comes necessarily from human nature. The world's great age does not begin anew nor do the golden years return. Mixed sorrow and joy are the portion of fallen man. What cannot be cured must be endured and whining never did anyone any good. If you do not expect of it more than ever it professed to give, *"après tout, c'est un monde passable."*

I have spoken of Toryism as if it were one among a number of competing political creeds. Such language is inevitable, yet it is not wholly just. For there is a fundamental cleavage between Toryism and any of the aspects of modern Liberalism. The Liberal programme speaks of man as it would like him to be. The Tories, from Chaucer to Johnson, speak of him as he is. They accept life. Their spirit is the spirit of St. Thomas à Kempis, who wrote, "Be not angry that you cannot make others as you wish them to be, since you cannot make yourself as you wish to be."

This acceptance, whatever its disadvantages, has at least one very large advantage. The Tory is by far the more entertaining conversationalist. For the Tory, when he speaks of the world, does really speak of the world. The Liberal, when he speaks of the world, speaks of the world as he would have it—that is to say, speaks of himself. The Tory describes; the Liberal preaches. Facts to the Liberal are but the stuff for sermons. To the Tory observation is an end in itself. Johnson sent Boswell to "explore Wapping"; he did not send him to reform it.

There is a bitter amusement to be got from reading to-day Macaulay's essays on Johnson and Goldsmith. To judge Macaulay by them would be most unfair. Macaulay was within his limits a very great man—a master of the word-picture. Yet even Homer nods and these two essays are two of the very few pieces of really bad work which he ever did. They are written in patronising confidence, as if in explaining eighteenth-century Toryism to the reader he was explaining a problem of archæology rather than of politics. He can never have thought that, when another hundred years had passed, his philosophy would be out of date and Johnson's and Goldsmith's would be still alive. Still less can it have occurred to him that a Professor of English Literature would remark in a casual aside, "A wiser man than Macaulay, James Boswell." Yet so it is. Eighteenth-century Toryism has more to say to us to-day than nineteenth-century Whiggery. Macaulay we read for his style and praise for his style, but he brings to us no comfort in our despairs. For comfort we must turn back to those nobler souls who challenged when they were moderate those evils of our life that have to-day grown monstrous, read the *Conduct of the Allies* or *Thoughts on the Late Transactions Concerning Falkland's Isle* for refuge from an Imperial madness, or turn too late to *The Deserted Village* while the unemployed are tramping in the streets.

In spite of their differences of temperament and of their many petty quarrels these two great men, Johnson and Goldsmith, kept always a high admiration for each other.

> "It may do me some honour to inform the public," wrote Goldsmith in his dedication to Johnson of *She Stoops to Conquer*, "that I have lived many years in intimacy with you. It may serve the interests of mankind also to inform them that the greatest wit may be found in a character without impairing the most unaffected piety."

When Boswell once noted as a curiosity that "Goldsmith has acquired more fame than all the officers of the last war who were not generals," "Why, sir," answered Johnson, "you will find ten thousand fit to do what they did before you find one who does what Goldsmith has done." On Goldsmith's death he wrote upon him, as all know, the very generous epitaph, *"Nullum fere scribendi genus non tetigit, nullum quod tetigit non ornavit";* and in a letter to Langton reporting his death paid the just and discriminating tribute of nobleness to nobleness.

> "He had raised money and squandered it by every artifice and acquisition of folly and expense. But let not his frailties be remembered; he was a very great man."

It is important to realise the amazing generosity of Johnson's praise of Goldsmith, a praise to which he returned again and again. The more true it is that Johnson overrated the importance of this knack of expressing oneself clearly, which is a convenient accomplishment but has in it nothing of nobleness, the more is his generosity to be praised. During their lifetime, Johnson and Goldsmith were thought of as Dr. Major and Dr. Minor to each other. To-day there has been a just reaction from that verdict, and it is generally admitted that there was a delicacy in Goldsmith's mind and style which Johnson could never rival. It is Johnson who is largely responsible for the reversal of that verdict, who, at a time when all the world was saying that Goldsmith was a mere echo of himself, with justice and generosity and honesty clamoured that this was by no means so, but that Goldsmith had written as he himself could never hope to write.

I remember once hearing someone say of Goldsmith that he had no respect for a man who did not live up to his professed principles. Surely a man who does live up to them must be, as Aristotle would have said, "either a beast or a god." For most of us, if we live up to our principles, it does not say very much for our principles. "Sir, are you so grossly ignorant of human nature," Johnson once asked—and, what is better, asked it of Macaulay's grandfather—"as not to know that a man may be very sincere in good principles without having good practice?"

Delicious and characteristic is Sir John Hawkins' comment on this. "Had his acquaintance lain at this time, as in the latter part of his life it did," writes the delightful knight, "with persons of rank and condition, he might have formed different notions on the subject."

It lay, instead, with Goldsmith. Now Goldsmith was not a good man (though he was not a very bad one), but at least he always knew that he was not a good man. He never called wrong right because he had done it. If you like, you may say that his practice did not conform with his principles. More important is it that he would never drag down his principles to make them conform with his practice.

Johnson was no feminist. A woman preaching was to him "like a dog walking on his hind legs; it is not done well, but you are surprised to find it done at all." Mixed bathing "as they do at Bath" was "an instance of barbarity that he believed could not be paralleled in any part of the world." He desired to preserve that broad line which tradition had drawn between the functions of woman and of man rather than return to the customs of barbarism and to a period such as that of Jael, the wife of Heber the Kenite, when women played their part in public life. "Nature," he thought, "has given women so much power that the law has very wisely given them little."

Yet he was anything but a woman-hater. Rather did he pride himself on the gallantry of his behaviour in feminine society. Still it was natural that his style of life should be more suited to men than to women. It is rare to find a woman who takes much pleasure in the exercise of reason, while in that exercise Johnson himself found his chief pleasure. Therefore, though he was often in the company of women and made himself agreeable in that company—"he has more fun and nonsense and comical humour about him than almost anybody I ever saw," wrote Fanny Burney—only a few women, apart from his altogether peculiar "seraglio," came at all constantly into his life.

There was Fanny Burney, who lived to be the last survivor of his circle. There were also those two very virtuous "blue stockings," Hannah More and

Mrs. Montague, whom one is so willing to admire across a distance of one hundred and fifty years. These two ladies thought that they had discovered in a Mrs. Yearsley, a poor milkwoman of Bristol, a poetess whom the study of the Bible had enabled to "soar above Pindar and Æschylus," and collected between £500 and £600 for her benefit. Having collected it, they then refused to give it to her for fear that she would spend it on drink—as of course she would have done. Both these literary ladies were very noble women, but they certainly had the talent, even when they were giving pleasure, of giving it as if it were a sort of pain and of bestowing a favour with the air that "it hurt them more than it hurt you."

With Mrs. Montague Johnson's relations grew cooler after his *Life of Lyttleton* had revealed to her that he did not share her admiration for her flatterer. To Hannah More he remained faithful to the end.

Yet the woman with whom his name is most closely associated is she who was known in his day as Mrs. Thrale, afterwards as Mrs. Piozzi, and who has left us a record of Johnson's habits only inferior to those of Boswell and Fanny Burney. Mrs. Thrale—the "papilionaceous creature," as the absurd Carlyle calls her—was the wife of a wealthy brewer of Southwark, the Member of Parliament for that borough. The pair had first met Johnson at the house of Arthur Murphy, the dramatist, a common acquaintance. The friendship had prospered and in the end had become so close that Johnson had been invited to make of the Thrales' houses second homes for himself. Both at Streatham and at Southwark a room came to be set apart for him. For sixteen years he almost lived with them. The three travelled together to France, to Wales and to the West of England, and the arrangement only came to an end at last because of the death of Thrale. Johnson had not foreseen that this would make any difference to his position in Mrs. Thrale's house. But Mrs. Thrale thought otherwise, and soon afterwards the house was let and Johnson turned out of his room at Streatham. A little later Mrs. Thrale, to Johnson's intense disgust, married again to an Italian music-master, called Piozzi, and Johnson and she separated in a final quarrel.

Who was to blame for the quarrel has never yet been quite settled. Boswell, naturally enough, was very loud on Johnson's side, denouncing vigorously Mrs. Thrale's baseness. Modern opinion has been more charitable to her and some have been found to wonder, not that she broke with him at last, but that she bore with him for so long. His manners were no better in Mrs. Thrale's house than they had been in Mrs. Boswell's. Indeed they were worse. For, after sixteen years, Johnson had come, it seems, to behave there very much as if he were in his own home—to complain of the food, to invite guests himself and even to complain out loud of the guests whom Mrs. Thrale invited. He "ate," she said, "too dirtily for endurance." It is very easy to understand that these gaucheries, which she could tolerate while her husband was still alive, might become quite intolerable when she was a widow. Johnson himself had written, in his *Life of Pope,* "It had been well observed that the misery of man proceeds, not from any single crash of overwhelming evil, but from small vexations continually repeated." How much more true is this of the misery of woman!

Nor do I think that anyone not entirely the victim of *lues Boswelliana* will find himself able to blame Mrs. Thrale very much. Even if there were no other evidence, the proprietary way in which Johnson tried to prevent her second marriage, the outrageous letter that he wrote to her when he heard that that marriage had taken place, would go far to prove that her conduct was very necessary if she was to keep for herself any chance of happiness. He wrote, it is true, a second and milder letter, but it was not, as it should have been, a letter of outspoken apology.

At the same time I am not willing to acquit Mrs. Thrale entirely. If, as she says, Johnson was the noblest man whom she ever knew, then she had no business to write the book which she did write; for the picture which that book gives is not the picture of a noble man. It is a malicious book. Its anecdotes are almost always malicious and often, where they can be tested, inaccurate. Boswell, whatever his defects, was a marvellously accurate reporter. Of his book, Reynolds, who had no especial reason to be biassed one way or the other, said that "every word might be depended upon as if given on oath." And many of Mrs. Thrale's anecdotes reappear in a form slightly different, and always more favourable to Johnson, in Boswell.

Besides, the Johnson whom Mrs. Thrale turned out of doors was a dying man. In spite of the excuses of an uneasy conscience, Mrs. Thrale knew that he was a dying man, and that she was the only person who could nurse him.

Were I to run through all the interesting people whom Johnson ever met, this chapter would become little more than a catalogue of eighteenth-century literary London. Among Johnson's acquaintances are some of whom our knowledge is tantalisingly small—Phil. Jones, for instance, whom, as I have already said, "loved beer and did not get very forward in the Church"; "Mr. F. Lewis," of whom recorded history is, "Sir, he lived in London and hung loose upon society"; Dr. Dodd, the King's chaplain, of whom a shocked contemporary records that he at one time "even descended so low as to become the editor of a newspaper," but who afterwards reformed his character and finished by merely being hanged for forgery; Henderson, of whom Johnson said, "I never did the man an injury, but he would persist in reading his tragedy to me"; Dudley Long, whose character Johnson summed up in the phrase, "He fills a chair," and who, when asked by Gibbon what Sheridan's comment had been on the *Decline and*

Fall, replied with the pleasing vagueness, "Oh, he said something about your voluminous pages"—a remark worthy to be classed with the Duke of Gloucester's, "Another damned thick book! Always scribble, scribble, scribble, eh, Mr. Gibbon?"; Santerre, the French brewer whom the Revolution was going to find at the head of the National Guard at King Louis's execution, of whom his enemies wrote

> Ci gît le général Santerre,
> Qui n'eût de Mars que la bière,

and his friends asked why he should not be guillotined "like other generals."

More extraordinary than all these, perhaps, was George Psalmanazar, a Frenchman who passed himself off as a Japanese convert to Christianity and for some years deceived all England. At that time "he thought it no sin . . . to eat human flesh, but owned it was a little unmannerly." Later he repented of his deception, altered his diet to that of "ten or twelve drops" of opium "in a pint of punch," and finished his days in an odour of almost incredible sanctity. Johnson "used to go and sit with him in an ale-house," and —such was his respect for his character—would "as soon have thought of contradicting a bishop."

Others—Wilkes, Gibbon, Wesley, Paoli—were well known, important and interesting people, but they were not primarily Johnsonians. We must here omit them. There remains one man without the mention of whom an essay on Johnson would be ridiculous.

James Boswell, Macaulay would have us believe, was little better than a half-wit. And, characteristically overdrawn as Macaulay's picture is, yet it is certain that, of all the many eminent men into whose company Boswell forced himself at one time or another, no one ever dreamed that he would compete with them for the verdict of posterity. His admission into the Literary Club, for instance, was only obtained by Johnson's announcement that he would blackball every other candidate until Boswell was elected.

Yet it seems, from the interesting researches of Dr. McNair Wilson, that it is not only because of his *Life of Johnson* that historians should be interested in Boswell. Before he became Johnson's pet-dog he had travelled in Corsica and had toyed with a fantastic plan for making the Old Pretender king of that island—for whose advantage it is hard to say. Anyway, he had played there to General Paoli a game very similar to that which he was afterwards to play to Johnson.

> "He came to my country," Paoli told Fanny Burney in his broken English, "and he fetched me some letter of recommending him; but I was of the belief that he might be an impostor, and I supposed in my mind that he was an espy; for I look away from him and in a moment I look to him again and I behold his tablets. Oh, he was to the work of writing down all I say. Indeed I was angry."

James Boswell

His experiences and a panegyric upon the virtues of the Corsicans—virtues which, as he later admitted, he largely invented to suit his own pleasure—Boswell afterwards published. Johnson got sick to death of Corsica, of which he advised Boswell to "empty his head." And Boswell pestered his friends, such as Temple, to repeat to him any praise of the book that they might hear. The book fell, in the days of his strong Corsican patriotism, into the hands of young General Buonaparte, who was much impressed by it and confessed a debt to it for some of his political ideas. To have been admired in the flesh by Samuel Johnson and in print by Napoleon Bonaparte is a double claim to distinction which makes one who tries to dismiss such a man as a naïve fool look himself very naïve.

Yet it cannot be denied that Boswell did possess very many of the superficial characteristics of a fool—indeed, was a fool, though not a mere fool. For he had a quality which was invaluable in the biographer and often ridiculous in the man—a lack of superficial self-respect. He "had genius," as his kinsman, Adam Smith, wrote, "but wanted ballast to counteract his whim."

Take the following if you would see the sort of man that he was:

"At Mr. Tytler's I happened to tell that one evening a great many years ago, when Dr. Hugh Blair and I were sitting together in the pit of Drury-lane play-house, in a wild fit of youthful extravagance I entertained the audience prodigiously by imitating the lowing of a cow."

Not content, he must add in a footnote:

"I shall not withhold any part of this story, however ludicrous. I was so successful in this boyish frolic that the universal cry of the galleries was 'Encore the cow! Encore the cow!' In the pride of my heart I attempted imitations of some other animals, but with very inferior effect. My reverend friend, anxious for my fame, with an air of the utmost gravity and earnestness addressed me thus: 'My dear sir, I would confine myself to the cow.' "

If that does not content you, add to it the account which he has left us of his behaviour on board ship in a storm.

"As I saw them all busy doing something I asked Col with much earnestness what I could do. He with a happy readiness put into my hand a rope which was fixed to the top of one of the masts, and told me to hold it till he bade me pull. If I had considered the matter I might have seen that this could not be of the least service; but his object was to keep me out of the way of those who were busy working the vessel and at the same time to divert my fear by employing me and making me think that I was of use. Thus did I stand firm to my post while the wind and rain beat upon me, always expecting a call to pull my rope."

He composed an *Ode to Tragedy, by a Gentleman of Scotland,* and dedicated it to "James Boswell, Esq.," writing in the dedication, "I, sir, who enjoy the pleasure of your intimate acquaintance, know that many of your hours of retirement are devoted to thought." He then published an explanation of what he had done.

We have most of us at one time or another made fools of ourselves. In emergencies we have been but a nuisance to be kept out of the way. Yet we are not eager to publish our idiocy to the world. Boswell, the great servant of truth, never shrank from her to save his own shame. He loved truth as if she were a person and in her service he was willing to accuse himself of things much worse than silliness. Some of his confessions to Temple remind one almost of Rousseau. Yet between Boswell and Rousseau there was a great difference. Rousseau confessed to wrong because he did not know the difference between it and right. Boswell confessed to wickedness and folly, but he never called folly wisdom nor excused wickedness by the plea that passion was irresistible.

He was the most unashamable celebrity-hunter. Why a person was celebrated he cared not at all. Whigs and Tories, kings and revolutionaries, bishops and barmaids—all were equally grist to his amazing mill. He was pleased to be in the company of Johnson or Paoli or Rousseau or David Hume. He was as pleased to be in that of Mrs. Rudd, a prostitute, who, as I have said, in the *cause célèbre* of the day had saved her life by turning King's evidence against her paramour. He rode to Tyburn in the cart with a murderer. When he could not be the chaperon of Rousseau, he was almost as pleased to be the chaperon of Rousseau's mistress. Nor, when he had gained his introductions, had Boswell any shame about the methods which he would employ for collecting the *bons mots* of the great.

If you would have a laugh at one of the greatest and most lovable of all books, you cannot better get one than by reading Alexander Chalmers's *Lesson in Biography,* which is among the most exquisite and most neglected of all prose parodies in our language. Of Boswell's behaviour in Johnson's presence Fanny Burney has left an admirably vivid description. When Johnson was at the table with him he would frankly neglect all the rest of the company. The note-book would come out. He would edge up nearer and nearer to Johnson, until at last he would be sharply ordered back to his place like a dog.

Once, Fanny Burney records, Boswell found to his disgust that she, and not he, had been placed next to Johnson. Unabashed, Boswell fetched his chair from its place and set himself down just behind Johnson.

> "His eyes goggled with eagerness; he leant his ear almost on the shoulder of the Doctor; and his

mouth dropped open to catch every syllable that might be uttered; nay, he seemed not only to dread losing a word but to be anxious not to miss a breathing. And there he remained until Johnson happened to turn and see him and shouted an ill-pleased 'What do you do there, sir? Go to the table, sir!' "

If Boswell could think of nothing sensible to say, he would keep the conversation going by questions almost idiotic, in the hope that even idiocy might stimulate a memorable reply. For, as he once said of himself in a curious poetical composition:

> This maxim, he says, you may see,
> We can never have corn without chaff;
> So not a bent sixpence cares he
> Whether with him or at him you laugh.

"If, sir," he once asked for want of anything better to ask, "you were shut up in a castle and a new-born baby with you, what would you do?"

Sometimes his inquisitiveness was more than Johnson could bear. "I will not be baited with what and why. Why is a cow's tail long? Why is a fox's tail bushy?" Or, "Sir, you have but two subjects, yourself and me. I am sick of both."

"Pray, sir," said Boswell, "can you tell me why an apple is round and a pear pointed?"

"Would not such talk make a man hang himself?" commented Johnson in reporting it.

"A poem on what?" Boswell once asked in rhetorical scorn concerning the *Dunciad*.

"Why," said Johnson, "on dunces. It was worth while being a dunce then. Ah, sir, hadst thou lived in those days!"

At another time Boswell pompously presumed to express his argument by a trite quotation from *Hamlet*.

"Nay, if you are to bring in gabble, I'll talk no more. I will not, upon my honour," snapped out Johnson.

Johnson objected to Boswell's publishing one of his letters. Boswell asked if he might publish it after Johnson's death.

"Nay, sir, when I am dead you may do as you will," answered Johnson, who cared no more than does any sensible man for the verdict of posterity.

Macaulay complains that, among all the opinions of Boswell of which we have record, not one gives evidence of sense or understanding. Napoleon at any rate, it seems, did not agree with him. Yet for the more part, it is certainly true, Boswell's opinions were but the echo of Johnson's. Boswell is one of the most quoted of authors. Yet it is only his quotations that are quoted. There is no fine, purple, original Boswell. Where he differed from Johnson, it was usually from an ambition to out-Johnson even Johnson in his prejudices. Thus he sometimes carried Toryism one step farther than Johnson would have carried it. He defended the slave-trade. So devoted was he to feudal principles that even in the eighteenth century he would not have allowed land to descend through a female.

On the other hand it must not be forgotten, as Mr. Bailey has reminded us, that on three questions at least—the American quarrel, the Middlesex election and Gray's poetry—the verdict of posterity is with Boswell and against Johnson.

For the most part his habits accommodated themselves very well to those of Johnson. Between them was only one striking difference. Neither Johnson nor Boswell was capable of moderate drinking. Boswell took refuge from his incapacity in intoxication, Johnson in abstention. Concerning his lapses from sobriety Boswell was pleasantly frank. One conversation of Johnson's at any rate—that which took place one night at the Bishop of St. Asaph's—is lost to us because Boswell was too drunk to remember it, and we may suspect that there are many more which have suffered from a similar oblivion. With a certain self-satisfaction he prints a poem of apology, which he wrote to Miss Monckton, afterwards the kleptomaniac Countess of Cork, for the condition in which he had presented himself before her on the previous night. There is something engagingly impersonal in his remarks that "intoxication might happen at a time to any man," and he writes of himself with truth as "a lover of wine and therefore curious to hear whatever is remarkable concerning drinking."

"After supper," he records in the *Journal of a Tour to the Hebrides,* "Dr. Johnson told us that Isaac Hawkins Browne drank freely for thirty years and that he wrote his poem, *De Animi Immortalitate,* in some of the last of these years.—I listened to this with the eagerness of one who, conscious of being himself fond of wine, is glad to hear that a man of so much genius and good thinking as Browne had the same propensity."

He records as a mere maxim of prudence Johnson's dictum that "a man who had been drinking freely should never go into a new company. He would probably strike them as ridiculous though he might be in unison with those who had been drinking with him."

From his letters to Temple, his clerical friend and the grandfather of the Archbishop of Canterbury of that name, it would seem that the problem of women was no less of a diffculty to him than was that of wine. Though he looked "with horror on adultery," nevertheless he kept "a sweet little mistress" who had been deserted by her husband, and even after his own marriage was able to "unite little fondnesses" for other ladies "with perfect conjugal love."

It was one of his whims to affect exaggerated sensibility. He would pretend to outdo Johnson in fits of melancholia. Music, he claimed, produced in him "alternate sensations of pathetic dejection so that I was ready to shed tears and of daring resolution so that I was ready to rush into the thickest of the battle."

"Sir," brutally replied the unmusical doctor, "I should never hear it if it made me such a fool."

It would be very easy to make a catalogue of the virtues and characteristics which Boswell did not possess. The temptation—a temptation to which Macaulay fell—is to imagine that when you have made such a list you have done with Boswell. Yet, as anyone who has ever tried it must realise, not every fool can give us in a few sentences the gist of a conversation. It is time to be done with those two silly paradoxes, of which the one would have it that Johnson created Boswell, the other that Boswell created Johnson. It is rare to find a man who can tell the truth. It is rare to find a man who can bear to have the truth told about him. By one of the great chances of literature Boswell was a man of the first class, Johnson of the second. When all is said and done, the best way to get to know the world is to live in it. The next best is to break your leg and read Boswell's *Life of Johnson* in bed.

Boswell was neither a thinker nor a poet, but he was a thing only less rare than these—a Benvenuto Cellini who told the truth. He was, I suppose, the greatest of all reporters; Herodotus is his only competitor. Nor was he merely the reporter of conversations. He was more than their reporter, for he was also their originator.

After the deaths of Johnson and his wife there was

no one left to check the vices of Boswell's character. He sank rapidly and found at last the grave of a sodden recluse. He had been repudiated by most of his friends. He was all but disowned by his children. His countrymen raised no monument to his glory. Yet, deserted, dishonoured, unnoticed, he has left behind him a name which will certainly survive so long as there survives among men any curiosity upon the manners and inhabitants of the past. He staked everything upon that very odd business, posthumous fame, and such a victory, for what it may be worth, he has very gloriously won.

Such were some of the company which talked away those last years before the enormous shock of revolution fell upon the world. They were great men, far greater than either the complacency of Macaulay or the ranting of Carlyle could ever guess. The daylight of the religious wars of the seventeenth century and of the Jacobites was done. It had been followed by an age of the evening, an age of candlelight. How astonishingly vividly Boswell has made all those old scenes live—the company and the talk and the wigs and the tea and the snuff; and in the middle, towering over all, a gigantic figure, gigantic physically, as gigantic in soul, a man who, "gloriously of our clay," seems to stand almost as a personification of the spirit of man, who took to himself, perhaps more completely than any other that ever lived, the old tag of *"Homo sum, et humani nihil . . . !"*

We must be careful of our distinctions. *"Humani*

nihil a se alienum putabat." Johnson, as has been said, loved many people whom the conventions of society, at any rate, dub bad people. But he never loved badness. He loved not the badness but the goodness in them, a goodness which they had perhaps in perversity concealed from the world but which they had been unable to conceal from Samuel Johnson.

I have spoken in an earlier place of how he boasted of the love of Bet Flint, a drunkard, a thief, and a harlot. Now Johnson was not the man to be carelessly indifferent to morals. No one ever accused him of that. Yet when, later in the same conversation, he had occasion to compare another woman with Bet Flint, he did so to her disadvantage, saying "she had not quite the same stock of virtue nor the same stock of honesty as Bet Flint." No man nor woman could sink so low that Johnson could not find goodness in them. He would, to borrow a phrase which Mr. Chesterton has used of Browning, "walk into the foulest of thieves' kitchens and accuse men publicly of virtue."

CHAPTER V

JOHNSON AND LIES

After he had received his pension, Johnson's literary activity came almost to an end. He wrote indeed a few pamphlets, under the influence of gratitude to the Government and his hatred of Whigs. They are pamphlets which, though they quite lack the great strength of Swift, yet are a good deal better than it is the fashion to make out. For Johnson was a political philosopher rather than a politician; yet, though he did not very well understand the workings of practical politics, he was unable to write without reasoning. Apart from them his only other literary works of any importance were the *Journey to the Western Islands,* which appeared in 1774, and the *Lives of the Poets,* which appeared in 1781.

Of his life during these years we might possibly know more were it not for the destruction of the mysterious two "quarto MS. volumes"—note-books of Johnson's own writing—into which Boswell one day peeped, of which Johnson said that, had Boswell stolen them, he "would have gone mad," one of which Sir John Hawkins afterwards got hold of, and both of which, when he had recovered the purloined one, Johnson then burnt. Of those quartos we shall now never know the contents. For these years we must make do with the account from the pen of Dr. Maxwell, an Irish friend who had made Johnson's acquaintance as far back as 1754.

Maxwell would call upon him at twelve o'clock in the morning and would generally find him either still in bed or else at tea and declaiming to a circle of friends. The declamation continued until dinner-time, when he would sally out either to a friend's house or else to a tavern. There would follow dinner and further declamation and, when dinner and declamation were done, he would transfer to another friend's house where there would be declamation and tea. Thence home to Miss Williams and more tea, and to bed in the small hours of the morning. The routine is tolerably simple.

It was saved from monotony by the variety of the conversation, which, except for tea, was now really Johnson's only pleasure. But of his conversation during these first pensioned years we have unfortunately very little record. The great recorder had not yet appeared.

Boswell, as has already been said, was the most unashamed of lion-hunters. He himself speaks with engaging and unabashable snobbery of "my desire of being acquainted with celebrated men of every description." He hunted all celebrities impartially, shamelessly and with entire indifference to the reason for which they might be celebrated.

> "I hope," he said, "in defence of that propensity in my disposition . . . it does not deserve so hard a name as either forwardness or impudence. If I know myself, it is nothing more than an eagerness to share the society of men distinguished either by their rank or their talents and a diligence to attain what I desire."

"I have the happiness," he said at another time, "of being able to contemplate with extreme delight those distinguished spirits by which God is sometimes pleased to honour humanity."

Naturally such a man was anxious to be introduced to Dr. Johnson, even if he seems, in his anxiety, to have had no idea that he was doing more than adding one to a bag. He first tried to arrange for an introduction through old Sheridan, the father of Richard Brinsley. The choice of agent was not happy, for Johnson had the lowest opinion of old Sheridan.

> "Why, sir, Sherry is dull, naturally dull," he had once said, "but it must have taken him a great deal of pains to become what we now see him. Such an excess of stupidity, sir, is not in nature."

A young man could not well have come to Johnson with a worse introduction. And it was fortunate for Boswell, and by consequence fortunate for us who are posterity, that these first intrigues came to nothing.

It was, as all know, at the house of Davies, the actor-bookseller, that the first famous meeting took place. "He is only a bur," Goldsmith used afterwards to explain of Boswell. "Tom Davies flung him at Johnson in sport, and he has the faculty of sticking."

Davies was an actor, who had been driven from the stage, it was said, by a cruel line in Churchill's *Rosciad*:

> He mouths a sentence as curs mouth a bone.

He then set up as a bookseller, and, falling upon hard times, was foolish enough to publish a "pirate" edition of Johnson's works. Johnson, at first angry, said that he would "storm and bluster a little," but was so moved by Davies's apology and his misery that he characteristically finished, not by a threat of legal proceedings, but by saying that "Thrale and I must do something for Tom Davies." When Davies went bankrupt, Johnson collected money to buy back his furniture and induced Sheridan to give him a benefit night at Drury Lane.

Davies's shop was at No. 8 Russell Street, Covent Garden, and thither on an important day—Monday, the 16th of May, 1763—it so happened that Boswell went to drink tea with Mr. and Mrs. Davies. As he sat there, it chanced that Johnson came in. What Boswell had failed to obtain by intrigue he obtained by luck.

Davies introduced the two, Boswell whispering

nervously to him as he did so, "Don't tell him where I come from."

> " 'From Scotland,' cried Davies roguishly.
>
> " 'Mr. Johnson,' said I, 'I do indeed come from Scotland, but I cannot help it!' . . .
>
> " 'That, sir, I find is what a very great many of your countrymen cannot help,' answered Johnson."

Later in the conversation Johnson happened to say to Davies, "What do you think of Garrick? He has refused me an order for the play for Miss Williams because he knows that the house will be full and that an order would be worth three shillings."

Boswell, eager to insert himself into the conversation, butted in with: "Oh, sir, I cannot think Mr. Garrick would grudge such a trifle to you."

Johnson, as has already been said, would have none criticise Garrick but himself.

"Sir," he answered, "I have known David Garrick longer than you have; and I know no right you have to talk to me on the subject."

For most men two such snubs would probably have been sufficient. Even the irrepressible Boswell admits that "had not my ardour been uncommonly strong and my resolution uncommonly persevering, so rough a reception might have deterred me for ever from making any farther attempts." We are fortunate in his ardour and his perseverance.

Such is the common version—that is to say, Boswell's version of the meeting—and doubtless the true one. Murphy's is different, and subtly more humiliating.

> "Upon another occasion this writer"—i.e. Murphy—"went with him"—Johnson—"into the shop of Davis, the bookseller, in Russell Street, Covent Garden. Davis came running to him almost out of breath with joy:
>
> " 'The Scots gentleman is come, sir; his principle wish is to see you; he is now in the back-parlour.'
>
> " 'Well, well, I'll see the gentleman,' said Johnson.
>
> "He walked towards the room. Mr. Boswell was the person. This writer followed with no small curiosity.
>
> " 'I find,' said Mr. Boswell, 'that I am come to London at a bad time when great popular prejudice has gone forth against us North Britains; but when I am talking to you I am talking to a large and liberal mind, and you know that I cannot help coming from Scotland.' " 'Sir,' said Johnson, 'no more can the rest of your countrymen.' "

From that time Boswell and Johnson began to meet with some frequency. They had in common, if little else, at least that kind of love of life which took the form of a love of London. To Johnson "Fleet Street has a very animated appearance, but I think that the full tide of existence is at Charing

Cross." And Johnson admitted that he had never come across anyone who had "such a gust for London" as had Boswell.

"Is not this very fine?" Johnson one day asked Boswell in Greenwich Park.

"Yes, sir," answered Boswell, "but not equal to Fleet Street."

"You are right, sir," said Johnson.

Yet it was some time before Boswell had at all perfectly learnt what sort of remarks could be safely made to Johnson and in what sort of moods they might be made. One day, early in their acquaintance, he badly put his foot into it. He repeated as a joke a saying of Hume that Johnson would be willing to stand before a battery of canon in order to restore Convocation to its full powers. To Johnson jokes against institutions of the Church and jokes by Hume were equally distasteful.

"And would I not, sir?" he thundered out in fury against poor Boswell.

Hume's especial virtue—that he reduced to absurdity Locke's theory that "all knowledge comes from experience"; that he showed that, if we do not know before we experience, then we can neither experience nor can we know, and thus proved a blind alley to be such—Johnson was ill fitted to appreciate, while to him Hume's mixture of Toryism and infidelity was particularly distasteful. His mind was irritated by the impertinence of apostacy, and Hume's tolerant and gentle scepticism, which led him to write to an atheist about to take Anglican orders, that "it was paying too great a respect for the vulgar to pique oneself on sincerity," was in many ways both more offensive and more dangerous than fighting anti-clericalism.

That a man should be wrong for the wrong reasons was bad. That he should be right for the wrong reasons was far worse. Hume, Johnson was always at pains to point out, was only a Tory by chance. No man could be a Tory by reason if he repudiated the Source of all reason. For Johnson's constant contention was that irreligious virtue was a contradiction in terms. Johnson saw—what the Victorian agnostic refused to see—that it was absurd to abolish Christian metaphysics and yet expect society to put itself to the inconvenience of preserving Christian morals. Happiness is (and must be) the end of man, and, if there is no future life in which happiness and virtue are equated, then it is unreasonable to practise virtue. Therefore he argued that "the belief in immortality is impressed upon all men, and all men act under an impression of it, however they may talk, and though perhaps they may be scarcely sensible of it."

For this reason did it particularly madden him to hear men speak of the composure with which Hume met his death. This was the subject of the conversation, according to Sir Walter Scott, at the only known interview between Johnson and Adam Smith. The authenticity of the story, I am afraid, hardly bears investigation.

"Sir," said the lexicographer, "you lie."

"Sir," said the economist, "you are the son of a whore."

And the two great thinkers turned from one another and went each upon his elevated way.

Johnson had, as have all wise men, a prejudice for the traditional over the anti-traditional. If anything has been said or done or believed by the mass of mankind through many generations, and in many different climates and cultures, then it is likely that there is some sense in it. The appeal to tradition—the appeal which, not content to take only the votes of those who suffer from the arbitrary accident of existing, polls, like an astute Irish politician, the dead as well as the living—this is the most democratic of all appeals.

This appeal, in the riots of Year-One-itis, it was the main folly of the French Revolution to neglect, and the neglect has infected and weakened all our judgments until to-day. The support of tradition cannot, it is true, give the certainty of a mathematical demonstration. But, where such a demonstration is not possible, the wise man will not lightly quarrel with a proposition that has such a support. "If in books thus made venerable by the uniform attestation of successive ages any passages shall appear unworthy of that praise which they have formerly received, let us not immediately determine that they owe their reputation to dullness or bigotry, but suspect at least that our ancestors had some reasons for their opinions and that our ignorance of those reasons makes us differ from them," wrote Johnson; and he sneered at Hume, "who has so much conceit as to tell all mankind that they have been bubbled for ages and he is the wise man who sees better than they."

Johnson therefore was rightly suspicious of any new opinion. If it was true, he felt that it would certainly have been held before.

> "A new manner," he cried. "Buckinger had no hands, and he wrote his name with his toes at Charing Cross for half a crown a piece; that was a new manner of writing."

Yet tradition, though it supplied Johnson with the healthy mind which enabled him to reject a mere novelty, did not, it must be confessed, always supply him with the argument with which to refute it. Sometimes his want of argument was at least partly compensated for by aptness of comparison. Take, for instance, his opinion on a woman preaching, or on Wesleyans at Oxford, or on a *congé d'élire,* which "is such a recommendation as if I should throw you out of a two-pair of stairs window and recommend you to fall soft," or that superb piece of vulgar back-chat with which he answered the abuse that was hurled at him by a Thames boatman, "Sir, your wife, under pretence of keeping a bawdy house, is a receiver of stolen goods."

At other times his refutation was less happy. Rightly he felt that Bishop Berkeley's idealistic metaphysics were too original to be at all likely to be true, and most people would to-day, I suppose, agree that they avoided difficulties rather than met them. Yet when Johnson struck his foot against a rock and cried, "I refute Berkeley thus," it was clear that he had understood neither the difficulties nor the metaphysics.

Everyone is always speaking of Johnson's prejudice against the Scotch. Johnson himself did not take his own prejudice too seriously. He was very capable of laughing at it. In the *Journey to the Western Islands* he records that at Montrose he and Boswell did not meet with such a reception as they might have expected. Johnson was about to revel in his prejudice and abuse of the innkeeper when "Mr. Boswell desired me to observe that the innkeeper was an Englishman, and I then defended him as well as I could." And, though he laughed at Scotch poverty, yet he paid to that poverty the very noble compliment of saying that "there are more gentlemen in Scotland than there are shoes." Yet certainly the prejudice was really there.

Whether or not the reason why it first came into his mind was, as Sheridan suggested, that the Scotch betrayed Charles I, the reason why he allowed it to remain there is clear enough. Whether the Scotch of his day had the quality which he accused them of having I cannot say, but that, if they did have it, he was right to dislike that quality is very certain. What he objected to in the Scotch was that they lied.

There are two kinds of liars. There is the liar

who swears that he has given you half a crown when he has really only given you two shillings. Of such lying Johnson did not especially accuse the Scotch. But there is another and more fundamental lying, to-day so prevalent and so generally tolerated that to condemn it seems almost a pedantry and it is a hard task even to make people understand what it is. By this second kind of lying I mean a fundamental refusal to face reality. There are many men who would die sooner than cheat at cards and yet who do not think it at all dishonourable to delude the unemployed by telling them that the country will soon have recovered its foreign trade or to earn a few guineas by upsetting the religious faith of simple people with a string of sophistries to which they will gaily admit that they have never given five minutes of serious consideration.

Cardinal Newman has written that "man does not want" the truth, "and therefore will not have it and in consequence by every means tries to stifle its appeal." Of Johnson, at any rate, this could not be said. He demanded that a soul should love the truth and he loved it himself. As the saint longs for the Beatific Vision or the poet for Beauty—or, if you prefer it, as the drunkard fights for the whisky-bottle or the Shylock for his ducats—so did Johnson fight for truth. Whatever the cost might be, with very little illusion about what the cost would be, "though it slay me," yet he demanded to be given the truth. Nothing should stifle its appeal.

To some such a passion may see eccentric. We are apt to ask whether truth matters, and we mean by the question "Will the world come to an end if we do not bother ourselves with it?" No, it will not immediately do so. For there survives in us a certain force of tradition which prevents us from wholly living down to our mean philosophies. We who usually lie—as most of us usually do—are but the poor relations of the human family. We live by sponging on those few—the Aristotles, the Johnsons, and the Newmans—who have put "dear truth" above "dear friends," above the pleasant, above the profitable, above the journalist's cheque and above the politician's sweeping majority.

Johnson's complaint against the Scotch was then that their honesty was merely commercial honesty and not a fundamental honesty of the soul. The Scotch, he thought, were in a conspiracy to cheat the world. Nor would he join in the common praise of democratic Scotch education. For the education which the poor Scotch received was not, he thought, such as to train the philosopher and to teach him how to live in the reason but merely such as to equip him to climb high upon the ladder of life—to tempt him with delights which, if he should gain them, he would find to be but dust and ashes. It was but an affair of titbits and tag-ends. "Scotch learning," he said, "is like bread in a besieged town. Every man gets a mouthful but no man a bellyful." "They obtain a mediocrity of knowledge between learning and ignorance." It was very true of much of the Scotch education of his day; it is very true of much of the English education of this.

Whether Johnson was right or wrong about the Scotch I will not pretend to say. Burke has made it proverbially impossible to indict a whole nation, and, though Johnson himself did not at all feel the impossibility, I will take refuge behind it in order that I may preserve my Scotch friends. At the least there is one exception to this generalisation—one example of a Scotchman who really cared about telling the truth. His name was James Boswell.

In contrast to the Scotch Johnson set the Irish. In many ways his prejudice in favour of the Irish, if you choose to call it a prejudice, was both saner and more interesting than his prejudice against the Scotch. The Irish, as everyone knows, are in the superficial, commercial sense enormously less honest than the Scotch. Fundamentally, Johnson thought them more honest, and this readiness of theirs to describe life as it was he expressed in a characteristically humorous and cynical phrase. "The Irish," he said, "are a fair people; they never speak well of one another."

One can understand very little of English history if one does not constantly remember how the word "Tory" came to change its meaning at the time of the American and French Revolutions. To-day it is used as a mere synonym for Conservative and even sometimes for Ulsterman. Yet in the eighteenth century the Tory was the enemy of war, the enemy of Imperialism and, above all, the friend of the oppressed Irish. To Johnson the Irish were the nation who had fought for an English king against a Dutch usurper. Because he was a sort of Jacobite he was therefore a sort of Sinn Feiner.

He protested, against Whig tyranny, as that other great Tory, Swift, had protested before him. To defend the oppression was "to talk the language of a savage." Patriotism was to him "the last refuge of a scoundrel," and he defended the Irish claim to freedom, not because it was, but because it was not, a separatist claim. Ireland belonged to the province of Europe from which England had seceded. "The devil was the first Whig," and Whiggery was the denial of those principles upon which all ordered society was built. The tragedy of England was that the Whigs should have captured that country and be forcing upon Englishmen the destruction of normal life. It was abominable that they should demand to carry their plutocratic anarchy across St. George's Channel and impose it upon a saner people who did not want to have any of it. "Do not make an union with us, sir," he said to an Irishman in prophetic warning. "We should unite with you only to rob you."

Johnson has often been accused, and rightly accused, of insularity. At least he was never so insular as to think, as the nineteenth-century Englishman came to think, that Whig, parliamentary England was in any way a normal society, upon which all other societies must necessarily wish to model themselves. The Irish stood for the normal: the English were trying to force upon the Irish the abnormal.

In spite of his prejudice against the Scotch and his hatred of the country, Johnson in 1773 set out in Boswell's company for a tour of the Hebrides. Both Boswell and Johnson have left us, as is well known, their accounts of that trip.

Both books are in one way disappointing. Both Boswell and Johnson shared their century's insensibility to natural beauty. Loose talk often speaks as if industrialism destroyed our love of nature. The opposite is at least as nearly true. Our ancestors, to filch a friend's admirable phrase, disliked the Highlands because they were high. To them a mountain was too terrible to be thought beautiful. A man will not love the mountains until he is sure that he will not be lost in them. Only to us of the charabancs have mountains become sufficiently accessible to be friendly. We look on them to-day for the first time with all the kindness with which we are accustomed to look on conquered enemies. We praise them, for praise of the enemy is a luxury that can safely be indulged by those who are certain of victory.

The tour, and the journey to it, brought Johnson into the company of several interesting people. He stayed, for instance, at Kingsburgh with Flora Macdonald, the heroine of the '45, slept in the bed in which Prince Charlie had slept, and saw the sheet in which the Prince had lain and in which Flora herself was afterwards to be buried. He called on the eccentric Lord Monboddo. He was taken by Boswell to Auchinleck to visit his pupil's old father. The visit was not one of which the omens were very happy. The relations between Boswell and his father were not good, and one could not come worse to Auchinleck than by the "introduction" of "Jamie." In the old father's opinion, James was outrageously wasting his time by trapesing round after this absurd hero and, naturally enough, it was thought that the hero must be deliberately encouraging the hero-worship. "A dominie, mon, an auld dominie—he keeped a schule and caauld it an acaademy" had been all the information concerning Johnson's past life which it had been to the old man's curiosity to acquire.

Add to all this that he was a violent Whig and it can be seen that all Boswell's brazenness was required to arrange such a meeting. Nor was the meeting a success. All too soon the conversation came to politics and the Civil War.

"What had Cromwell done for his country?" shouted Johnson.

"God, doctor, he gart kings ken that they had a lith in their necks," answered old Boswell.

Boswell concludes the account of the meeting with the pious hope that the two have since met in a higher state, "where there is no room for Whiggism."

When in 1774 Johnson published his account of the Scotch tour, one of the consequences of publication was his famous controversy with James MacPherson concerning the authenticity of Ossian.

MacPherson had published shortly before a book which professed to contain the translation from the original Gaelic of the poems of Ossian, the manuscripts of which poems he had, he said, discovered in various Highland farmhouses. The authenticity of the poems was generally admitted but Johnson was an impenitent sceptic. He demanded that the original manuscripts be produced and, when MacPherson did not produce them, dubbed him a liar. MacPherson wrote Johnson a furious letter demanding a retractation. Johnson laid in a cudgel and replied:

> "Mr. James MacPherson, I have received your foolish and impudent letter. Any violence offered me I shall do my best to repel; and what I cannot do for myself the law shall do for me. I hope I shall never be deterred from detecting what I think a cheat by the menaces of a ruffian.
>
> "What would you have me retract? I thought your book an imposture; I think it an imposture still. For this opinion I have given my reasons to the public which I here dare you to refute. Your rage I defy. Your abilities since your *Homer* are not so formidable; and what I hear of your morals inclines me to pay regard not to what you shall say but to what you shall prove. You may print this if you will.
>
> "SAM. JOHNSON."

It is the fashion to say that, though Johnson was right in his accusation, he was only right by chance. He was led in the first place to doubt the authenticity by the extremely sceptical turn of his mind. In the second place Ossian's appeal was to those devotees of the cult of Nature which the new romanticism of Rousseau was then popularising and the cant of which Johnson always heartily hated.

Into the very large question of the legitimacy of the romantic appeal in art we can hardly enter here. Of Johnson's scepticism and his credulity it is worth saying a few things.

Macaulay started a fashion, which has since been followed by many others, of holding up Johnson to ridicule for the wild confusion of belief and unbelief which filled his mind. He refused to believe in an earthquake at Lisbon or that Boswell conversed by signs with some Esquimaux and made them understand his meaning. He was ready to believe in the Cock Lane ghost. His prejudices and credulities were, it is pretended, quite uncontrolled by reason or principle. A psychological theory has even been invented to explain him. It is said that a strong mind needs to be sceptical about a certain number of things and that Johnson therefore, having allowed himself to be superstitious where he should have been sceptical, had by recompense to be sceptical where he should have been believing.

The lack of balance is the more remarkable, we are told, because Johnson's was a sane, unenthusiastic, enquiring age, in which men shrank instinctively from belief in the extraordinary. But in an age in which the King of England accepted without hesitation the claim of one Mary Toft to have given birth to the lights and guts of a pig and to no less than fifteen rabbits the judgment requires surely a certain modification.

That Johnson believed some things which a sensible man should not have believed and refused to believe some others which a sensible man should have believed, I am prepared to admit. His was not a perfectly balanced mind. At the same time he was not, I fancy, such a fool as Macaulay made him out to be; and, if one considers all the instances of his credulity and incredulity, it is possible, I think, to see that his reason played a much larger part in the formation of his belief than is sometimes admitted.

A distinction is often missed. He did not credulously believe in second sight or the Cock Lane ghost. He was merely willing to discuss the possibility of second sight and to investigate the story of the ghost. That is to say, he was, as every sensible man should be, always very reluctant to say that any phenomenon was impossible. A thing to his mind was not impossible unless it implied some plain metaphysical impossibility. Ghosts, the king's evil, second sight, implied no such impossibility.

This distinction you will find drawn by Strahan, the Rector of Islington, in his Preface to Johnson's *Prayers and Meditations*. You will find it even better drawn by Boswell in the *Journal of a Tour to the Hebrides*.

> "As, on the one hand," Boswell explains of his master, "his faith in the Christian religion is firmly founded upon good grounds, so on the other he is incredulous where there is no sufficient reason for belief; being in this respect just the reverse of modern infidels who, however nice and scrupulous in weighing the evidences of religion, are yet so often ready to believe the most absurd and improbable tales of another nature, that Lord Hailes well observed a good essay might be written *Sur La Credulité Des Incredules*."

This is shrewd sense. Boswell is a very easy man to underrate.

Of a particular claim Johnson was then very sceptical. For that was a matter, not of metaphysical possibility, but of human evidence. And, as every police magistrate knows, it is extremely rare to find any man or woman capable of giving an accurate account of some incident even though he, or she, has no motive nor intention to pervert the facts. The teller of a story, even where he has no other temptation, has always the temptation to exaggerate in order that more attention may be paid to his story.

Johnson then never denied the possibility of the Esquimaux or of the earthquake at Lisbon. That would have been as silly as to deny the possibility of second sight. He merely asked, "Could Boswell pro-

Pembroke College, Oxford

duce certain evidence of the Esquimaux having understood him?" He merely argued that if a man comes and says that there has been an earthquake at Lisbon, one of two things must be true: either there has been such an earthquake or else the man is a liar. The second alternative was, to his mind, at least as likely to be true as the first. When the accumulation of evidence for the earthquake made it hardly possible that the whole story could be a fabrication, Johnson sensibly gave a grunt and believed.

Nothing could be more balanced than his weighing of the evidence for second sight in the *Journey to the Western Islands*, and he reaches in the end the conclusion, "I never could advance my curiosity to conviction, but came away at last only willing to believe"; or, as Peter Pindar, in a parody of Johnson, puts it somewhat more sharply:

> As for witches,
> Naught proves the non-existence of the bitches.

His opinion, sceptical and rational, upon departed spirits may be seen from one of the prayers which he composed concerning his dead wife:

> "O Lord, Governor of Heaven and Earth, in Whose hands are embodied and departed spirits, if Thou hast ordained the souls of the dead to minister to the living and appointed my departed wife to have care of me, grant that I may enjoy the good effects of her attention and ministration, whether exercised by appearances, impulses,

dreams or in any other manner agreeable to Thy government; forgive my presumption, enlighten my ignorance and, however meaner agents are employed, grant me the blessed influences of Thy Holy Spirit, through Jesus Christ Our Lord. Amen."

Boswell once argued with Johnson that, on his canons of probability, he ought to agree with Hume concerning miracles, "that it is more probable that witnesses should be deceived or lie than that miracles should happen." Johnson answered:

> "Why, sir, Hume, taking the proposition simply, is right. But a Christian revelation is not proved by miracles alone, but as connected with the prophecies and with the doctrines in confirmation of which the miracles were wrought."

That is to say, he did not believe the Christian metaphysics because he believed the Christian miracles, but rather believed the miracles because he believed the metaphysics.

Nothing is sillier than the polite fiction that most people normally tell the truth. To Johnson, lying—that is, the false description of incidents—was an almost universal trait. There was very little truth told in the world. "Sir, he lies," was the phrase always on Johnson's lips. Yet, that implied no wilful perversion. Where there was an intention to deceive the phrase was, "Sir, he lies, and he knows that he lies."

Johnson was a man of the world. He did not insist upon the verbal scrupulosity of a Quaker. It was a mistake to lie too much. But a certain amount of lying, he fully recognised, was a social necessity. When such a necessity arose, it was only important to know that you lied and not to deceive yourself.

> "Sir, clear your mind of cant," he told Boswell. "You may talk as other people do; you may say to a man, 'Sir, I am your most humble servant.' You are not his most humble servant. You may say, 'These are bad times; it is a melancholy thing to be reserved to such times.' You don't mind the times. You tell a man, 'I am sorry you had such bad weather the last day of your journey and were so much wet.' You don't care sixpence whether he is wet or dry. You may talk in this manner; it is a mode of talking in society; but don't think foolishly."

Certainly no one ever had a better opportunity to avoid doing so than had he who was the continual audience of Johnson's conversation.

CHAPTER VI

THE POETS AND THE DINNER-TABLE

Between 1777 and 1780 Johnson was occupied in writing his *Lives of the Poets*. They are not, I suppose, much read now. Yet Johnson had the knack, as he justly said of himself, of writing "trifles with dignity," and Byron, who, because he was overrated by his own age as a poet, is therefore underrated by ours as a critic, has praised them as "the finest critical work extant."

Nevertheless, most of the poets of whom Johnson wrote were not very interesting people even in their own lifetime and can to-day excite the curiosity of few. And where Johnson has a real poet about whom to write he is handicapped in his task by the disadvantage that he only very imperfectly knew what poetry was. He writes, for instance, of Waller, and never mentions his lyrics.

Yet this disadvantage, while causing him to miss the poet's poetry, often enabled him to see more clearly less important truths to which others have been blinded by their enthusiasm. He has been blamed for his prejudice against Gray. As a life, the life is certainly one of Johnson's least satisfactory.

Yet we to-day are at an unfair advantage over him. We have the benefit of two centuries of criticism to help us to spot a winner, and it is very easy to pretend that we would certainly have spotted him even without that assistance. Yet, after all, who is Gray? He wrote the "Elegy"—and Johnson praised it to the skies. Who reads anything else that he wrote? In the *Oxford Book of English Verse* there are of his, besides the "Elegy," a bit about a cat, a bit about the "Progress of Poesy," and an extract from the "Bard." Add to these the "Ode on Adversity" and that "Ode on a Distant Prospect" which the patriotism of old Etonians still contrives to keep fitfully alive. Does Gray honestly mean such an enormous amount to all of us that we need to be so unspeakably shocked at the Philistinism of Johnson, who did not very much care about him and characteristically said so? Such a poem as the "Bard" is a reasonably interesting story, reasonably interestingly told. There is nothing wrong with it; there is equally nothing right with it. Any man who knows his letters can tell in tolerable verse a story which will rhyme and scan. That Gray could do, but only a baker's dozen can do more, and Gray, who was in the dozen when he wrote the "Elegy," was not in it when he wrote the "Bard." It is right to be critical of Johnson's attempts at poetry; it is only fair to be as critical of the attempts of those whom he has criticised.

It is surely not perversity which makes me even wish that Johnson had been more offensive about

Gray than he was. He praised the "Elegy"—but, then, everybody praises the "Elegy." What the "Elegy" suffers from is lack of intelligent blame.

> Haply some hoary-headed swain may say,

is a silly line, and the more that one reads it the sillier it becomes.

> Approach and read (for thou canst read) the lay,

is an absurd bathos. I wish that Johnson had said so instead of taking refuge in praise.

Take again his criticisms of Milton.

A few things—a very few things—in poetry are settled. On ninety-nine poems out of a hundred the critic may say what he likes, and, if only he say it at all reasonably, we will listen to him. But if he tries to tell us that Shakespeare could not write sonnets or that the "Ode to a Nightingale" is not poetry we have done with him for a tedious fool, however well he write. "Lycidas" and Milton's sonnet:

> Methinks I saw my late espousèd saint,

are in this small class, and, when Johnson tells us that the former is a "disgusting" poem and that there is no merit in the latter, we are tempted to throw the book down in impatience. Yet even here Johnson can teach us much. He condemns "Lycidas" for its pastoral conventions, and, great as are the merits of "Lycidas," its pastoral conventions are not among them. Its pastoral conventions are ridiculous. It owes its greatness to its beauty, and he makes it easier for us to admire the beauty of its beauty who forces us to laugh at the absurdity of its absurdity.

Johnson says also that the poem bears no mark of sincere grief. Here, again, he is surely right, and there is one easy test of how right he is. When all is said and done with "Lycidas," how much do we know about Mr. Edward King?

Milton was a great poet, but no mistake could be worse than that of thinking that for that reason he has any other especial claim to our respect. He is a man easily underblamed, and Johnson might well have blamed him a little more. Of his opinions few were profound, many false and some disgusting. As a controversialist, he defended those opinions by methods that were always ill-mannered and often positively dishonest. His private character was not attractive. In his greatest poem he set out to "justify God's ways to man." That poem is almost the finest, if not the finest, blank verse that the world has ever known. To quote Dryden's generous praise, "This man cuts us all out, and the ancients too." Yet, as Thackeray unanswerably said, "Blank verse is not argument." If one considers it simply as a theological tract, "Paradise Lost" is a failure.

Take, for instance, the argument of the third book. Because man has sinned, somebody or other must be found to suffer for him. None of the angels are good enough to be willing to do so, and the Son alone is ready to offer Himself as a sacrifice. Now no one would maintain that justice would be especially promoted if, because a costermonger had eaten an apple which did not belong to him, the Prince of Wales was to go and get executed; nor, if the Son is not consubstantial with the Father, is there any sense in the Atonement. The Miltonic Son is not consubstantial. "By merit called My Son" is the phrase by which the Father is made to describe Him in "Paradise Regained," and, in case some should be found to argue that poets do not mean what they say, Milton left behind him the very prosaic prose of *De Doctrina Christiana* in order to leave no doubt of his opinion. Yet, if the Son, however superior to man, is in any way a limited Being, then clearly His Incarnation cannot of itself possibly recreate a broken relationship between the limited and the unlimited.

An Omnipotent God could certainly, had He wished, have readmitted man into the love of His desire by a mere "*Fiat*." "*Deus per suam omnipotentem virtutem poterat humanam naturam multis aliis modis reparare*," says St. Thomas. There could have been redemption with no sacrifice at all. And, if such a redemption was possible to God, it was clearly possible for Him to accept some smaller sacrifice as a satisfaction for the sins of the world. He might have accepted the sacrifice of Isaac. He might, as Milton would have it that He did, have accepted the sacrifice of the first of His creatures. But the whole world is not large enough to tell the difference between the faith of one who believed that this is what God did do and the Athanasian faith of such a man as Johnson who believed that God put Himself at one with His creatures, not by accepting the sacrifice of another, but, instead, by the sacrifice of Himself.

All this, it is true, does not matter to the poetry, if by poetry you mean merely word-music. Still it is as well every now and again to come across someone who bluntly says it. It is certain—and so obvious as to be hardly worth saying—that Milton could write better than Johnson. It is as certain that Johnson could think better than Milton.

With Milton, as with Gray, my regret is that Johnson did not say more. In estimating genius you cannot make up on the swings what you have lost on the roundabouts. If you have not praised a great man's greatness, you do not make up for it by praising his folly. If Johnson was unable to appreciate the goodness of Milton's poetry, I wish at any rate that he had been able to appreciate the badness of his philosophy.

There seems to be abroad a popular impression that Johnson deliberately set himself out to write down Milton by all means, fair or foul, because Milton was a republican and a regicide. That impression comes, I fancy, from Mark Pattison's *Life of Milton*. In a couple of pages of that extraordinary book we read, first, that:

> "Dr. Johnson, the most vigorous writer of the day, conspired with one William Lauder, a native

> of Scotland seeking fortune in London, to stamp out Milton's credit by proving him to be a wholesale plagiarist. Milton's imitations—he has gathered pearls wherever they were to be found—were thus to be turned into an indictment against him. One of the beauties of 'Paradise Lost' is, as has been already said, the scholar's flavour of literary reminiscence which hangs about its words and images. This Virgilian art in which Milton has surpassed his master was represented by this pair of literary bandits as thefts and held to prove at once moral obliquity and intellectual feebleness";

and, later, that, when Lauder's fraud was discovered, Johnson,

> "only guilty of indolence and party spirit, saved himself by sacrificing his comrade. He afterwards took ample revenge for the mortification of this exposure in his *Lives of the Poets* in which he employed all his vigorous powers and consummate skill to write down Milton."

The truth is that Lauder wrote *An Essay on Milton's Use and Imitation of the Moderns in His "Paradise Lost,"* in which he fraudulently and clumsily accused Milton of plagiarism. Johnson, accepting (let us readily admit it) Lauder's word with too little inquiry, wrote a preface to the essay and a postscript in which he took the opportunity to appeal for financial help for Milton's granddaughter.

In that postscript the man whom Mark Pattison accused of a conspiracy to "stamp out Milton's credit" wrote:

> "It is yet in the power of a great people to reward the poet whose name they boast and from their alliance to whose genius they claim some kind of superiority to every other nation of the earth; that poet whose works may possibly be read when every other monument of British greatness shall be obliterated; to reward him not with pictures or medals which, if he sees, he sees with contempt but with tokens of gratitude which he perhaps may even now consider as not unworthy the regard of an immortal spirit."

As soon as Johnson was convinced of Lauder's fraud, he did, it is true, "sacrifice his comrade"—would Pattison not have had him do so?—and forced from him a public confession and apology. In the work in which he is supposed "to have employed all his vigorous powers and consummate skill to write Milton down," whatever blunders he may have made as a critic, he yet wrote, "It has been therefore said without indecent hyperbole that in reading 'Paradise Lost' we reach a book of universal knowledge." He placed Milton second only to Homer among epic poets, and wrote that "his work is not the greatest of heroic poems, only because it is not the first."

Boswell has quoted the passage:

"Fancy can hardly forbear to conjecture with what temper Milton surveyed the silent progress of his work and marked his reputation stealing its way in a kind of subterraneous current through fear and silence. I cannot but conceive him calm and confident, little disappointed, not at all dejected, relying on his own merit with steady consciousness and waiting without impatience the vicissitudes of opinion and the impartiality of a future generation."

It is strange that a man of Mark Pattison's standing should have been guilty of such mean and unscholarly pages. It is to be regretted that he should have refused to Johnson "that impartiality of a future generation" which Johnson demanded for Milton.

The most interesting of the Lives is perhaps that of Savage, written thirty-five years before the rest and to which I have already referred. In it the reader will find little about poetry but a very interesting description of a very curious kind of life which Johnson knew from personal experience and of a very curious individual who lived that life and whom Johnson also knew.

The *Lives of the Poets* is unique among Johnson's works, for it is the only one of them which he did not write for money. What he did write it for is less easy to make out. No one could have had less illusion than he had about poets' lives. Of most of their lives he was well aware that the less said the better, while of nice distinctions between the merits of rival minor poets he said brutally, "Sir, there is no settling the point of precedency between a louse and a flea." "I wonder," he reasonably reflected, "that so many people have written who might have let it alone."

At least he did not allow his writing to interfere with his social life. And it is with conversation that these years were mainly occupied. Doubtless as a conversationalist he often, in the heat of the moment, said exaggerated things, little thinking that they would survive into cold print, be stared at, quoted, discussed one hundred and fifty years after his death. Sometimes he frankly argued for arguing's sake. Argument was a competition, and, as Sir Walter Raleigh has said, he loved a fight as heartily as he hated a quarrel. Garrick tells of his shouting out, "Why, sir, as to the good or evil of card-playing——" and then pausing for somebody to take the one side so that he might take the other. Beauclerk once asked him why Pope wrote a certain couplet. "Sir, he hoped it would vex somebody," answered Johnson with genial malevolence. It was a motive by which a proportion of his own remarks might be explained. He was well aware of the vices of his virtues.

> "To be frank," he wrote of Baretti to Mrs. Thrale, "he thinks is to be cynical and to be independent is to be rude. Forgive him, my dearest lady, the rather because of his misbehaviour I am

afraid he learnt part of me. I hope to set him hereafter a better example."

Yet on the whole it is remarkable how consistent with one another are his sayings. That a man should talk and be talked at for a generation, and at the end of it change his opinions so little, is very extraordinary. The explanation is partly, I suppose, that by this time he was growing slightly deaf.

When we think of Johnson at conversation we too easily think of the tyrant of the table, roaring down all opposition. Conceited people who do not find as much attention paid to them as they imagine themselves to deserve are apt to give to great conversationalists the reputation of bullies. Doubtless Johnson must have sometimes behaved in such a way as to deserve that reputation. Often, to quote a perfect phrase of Boswell, "he waited an opportunity to give the gentleman a blow of reprehension." He confessed to the fault himself. And, as Burke said, "It is well when a man comes to die if he has nothing worse to accuse himself of than some harshness in conversation." Yet it is a very partial picture which paints Johnson as merely a bully. Sir John Hawkins is none too favourable a witness. Of him Johnson said:

"As to Sir John, why, I really believe him to be an honest man at the bottom; but to be sure he is penurious, and he is mean, and it must be owned he has a degree of brutality and a tendency to savageness that cannot easily be defended."

Yet this Sir John says of Johnson, "He encouraged others, particularly young men, to speak, and paid a due attention to what they said." Such was certainly Johnson's own opinion concerning himself. All turns, I suppose, upon the meaning of the word "due." But it is astonishing that anyone who has read the *Memoirs of Fanny Burney* can find in the picture of the courtly, considerate, charming old gentleman the features of the habitual bully.

The marks of a Johnsonian *mot* are that it should be surprising, perhaps in the sense that it says something that people have never thought of before, but more frequently in the sense that it says what everybody has always known and acted upon, but the brutal expression of which the conventions of society usually avoid; that it should be concentrated as an epigram must be concentrated; that it should bear examination in the sense that the more you think of it the more meaning you see in it; that it should be opposed to cant.

The secrets of his greatness as a talker are, I think, two. In the first place he talked, as all good talkers do, on his companion's strong subject. "All discourse of which others cannot partake is not only an irksome usurpation of the time devoted to pleasure but, what never fails to excite very keen resentment, an insolent assertion of superiority and a triumph over less enlightened understandings." "Sir, Dr. Johnson would learn to talk of runts," was the merited rebuke doled out to the clergyman who complained that in the country no one could talk of anything but "runts."

No human activity was uninteresting to him. There was in him something universal. We cannot imagine an environment with which he would not have been able to cope. How poor a figure most of the literary men of the eighteenth century would have cut, let us say, at a League football match! Goldsmith would have been miserable; Burke bewildered, and every inch a philosopher; Boswell merely secondary; Reynolds would have painted it; Fielding would have understood the game. But Johnson I can well imagine in the paddock in front of the directors' box, blind, ignorant and yet entirely triumphant. "Sir," he would have said, "there was no obstruction. No, sir, it is not magnanimous that a penalty should be awarded where there has been neither insolence towards the referee nor prevarication towards the defenders." There is no other figure of the past whom one can so easily fit into any congregation of many men.

In the second place, Johnson never descended to mere cleverality. The manufacture of paradox and epigram is not very difficult once you get the hang of it, and it requires little effort. Certainly a man of Johnson's mental vigour could easily have invented a paradox and a sophistry with which to defend it every five minutes of his life, had he wished to do so. But for mere wit he had no respect. No one has ever been more witty at its expense.

> "He that had never any other desire than to fill a chest with money or to add another manour to his estate, who never grieved but at a bad mortgage or entered a company but to make a bargain, would be astonished to hear of beings known among the polite and gay by the denomination of wits. How would he gape with curiosity or grin with contempt at the mention of beings who have no wish but to speak what was never spoken before; who, if they happen to inherit wealth, often exhaust their patrimonies in treating those who will hear them talk; and if they are poor, neglect opportunities of improving their fortunes for the pleasure of making others laugh? How slowly would he believe that there are men who would rather risk a legacy than the reputation of a distich; who think it less disgrace to want money than repartee; whom the vexation of having been foiled in a contest of raillery is sometimes sufficient to deprive of sleep; and who would esteem it a lighter evil to miss a profitable bargain by some accidental delay than not to have thought of a smart reply till the time of producing it was past? How little would he suspect that this child of idleness and frolic enters every assembly with a beating bosom, like a litigant on the day of decision,

and revolves the probability of applause with the anxiety of a conspirator whose fate depends upon the next night: and at the hour of retirement he carries home under a show of airy negligence a heart lacerated with envy or depressed with disappointment; and immures himself in his closet that he may disencumber his memory at leisure, review the progress of the day, state with accuracy his loss or gain of reputation and examine the causes of his failure or success?"

> Eek Plato saith, whoso that can him rede,
> The wordes mote be cosin to the dede.

No man who had so much business with words ever remained so triumphantly their master as did Johnson. Look at the way in which even Shakespeare again and again lets words run away with him. In Johnson you can find no instance of that. Where he was wrong he was fundamentally wrong. Nobody ever tricked him on to the wrong side by decking out falsehood in some attractive phrase. I once asked a very able man why he admired Johnson, and he answered that it was because he had such an unprejudiced mind. Macaulay and Carlyle still rule over us sufficiently to make such an answer seem almost a wilful paradox, yet I am sure that it is a true and important judgment, and Leslie Stephen, a wiser man than Macaulay or Carlyle and one whom justice will place in the very first rank of writers of nineteenth-century English prose, said much the same thing.

Johnson had strong opinions, which muddle-headed people sometimes think to be the same thing as having prejudices. He hated Scotchmen and Whigs and Dissenters and Americans and all the rest. But for all these hatreds, just or unjust, he could give, and did give, very solid reasons. He could not, it is true, remember how he first came to dislike the Scotch: he could very well explain why he went on disliking them.

Every saying of Johnson is a temptation to a discursive essay. "There are," he told Strahan, the publisher, "few ways in which a man can be more innocently employed than in getting money." It was characteristic of Johnson to hate the cant of the simple life. He knew that the good things of life did add to its pleasure, and hated the dishonesty of those who denied this. "A man who does not mind his belly will hardly mind anything else," he said with patent falsity, and he advised people to "fix on some business where much money may be got and little virtue risked." It was always his custom somewhat to exaggerate the influence of money upon happiness. The reason for this exaggeration is clear and creditable. Johnson had both known real poverty himself and seen it in others. He knew what its misery was —the misery of not knowing where the next meal was coming from, or even whether there was going to be a next meal—and he rightly hated the humbug of those who would try to shrug away this misery with some quotation of a poet's phrase.

But his righteous hatred blinded him to the law of diminishing returns. It is true that man has certain material needs and that, if he has not the money with which to satisfy those needs, all the poetry and philosophy in the world will not make him happy. Even all the religion in the world will not make him happy unless he be one of those rare beings, like a St. Teresa, who can live daily in the conscious company of God. As Johnson said with enormous common sense:

> "Sir, all the arguments which are brought to represent poverty as no evil show it to be evidently a great evil. You never find people labouring to convince you that they may live very happily upon a plentiful fortune."

Yet it is false logic to argue from this that, the richer a man is, the happier he is. After he has satisfied his first material needs, there is indeed plenty left upon which he can spend his money and he can spend it in such a way as greatly to add to his happiness. Nevertheless the money which buys a cup of coffee after dinner clearly has less influence upon happiness than the money without which there would be no dinner at all. The law of diminishing returns, as I have said, very soon sets in, and to this Johnson was blind. "If £600 a year procure a man more consequence and, of course, more happiness than £6 a year, the same proportion will hold as to £6,000 and so on as far as opulence can be carried."

Yet the truth surely is that starving people certainly are not happy but that, from the man who has a secure living wage upwards, money has comparatively little effect upon happiness, except that very few people are happy if they are forced to accept a lower standard of living than that to which they have been accustomed. Among the working classes, among the middle classes, among the rich, among the very rich, there are happy and unhappy. Their happiness or unhappiness has, I fancy, very little to do with money. And men who "regulate all their conduct by the love of money" are, as Johnson says in the *Rambler,* "the meanest and cruellest of human beings."

The saying is not one of Johnson's most satisfactory. For it shirks a point—a fault of which he was not apt to be guilty. Obviously there is nothing wrong about "getting money" in itself. If someone walked into the room and offered me £5,000 a year on no conditions at all, I should be a fool if I did not accept. "For," as Johnson truly said, "*cœteris paribus,* he who is rich in a civilised society must be happier than he who is poor." The innocence or guilt is dependent upon how you are getting the money.

For the most part money must be made from business. The business may be merely fraudulent, whether in a technically legal or in a moral sense. Let us however suppose it legitimate. Then, if you really do create wealth, you are certainly an honest man and have a right to your money. But it will be very strange if, before you have acquired it, you have not become also a very dull and a very coarse one. For it is bad for the mind to be exercised continually upon material things. The Greeks were right to recognise that such exercise left a mark—and a degrading one—upon the character. And it is a lack of courage in the modern man which makes him so greedy for the products of industry that he is even willing to flatter the industrialist.

If you have got to make money you have got to make money, and someone must do the world's business. As Johnson said:

> "So many objections might be made to everything that nothing could overcome them but the necessity of doing something. No one would be of any profession as simply opposed to not being of it; but everyone must do something."

Yet some men are happier when they are idle and others happier when they are working, and it takes a very small proportion of the world's population to supply the material necessities of life. On the other hand, the world has more need of happy men than of industrious ones. We should not have been the gainers had Sir John Falstaff been sent to a lawyer's office or St. Francis kept to the study of the binomial theorem. As Stevenson said, "If a man cannot be happy without being idle, let him be idle." Energy and activity are necessary to lesser minds in order to save them from boredom. But there is a menace in the cult of action. One only does in order to be, and to rare and ample souls existence is sufficient. To such men as the old Greeks idleness was positive. Business was merely not having nothing to do. I daresay that it is true that idleness is bad for the character; but, then, so is business.

Johnson himself was well aware of the degrading effect of trade upon the character and put the point as well as it could be put:

> "There are," he said, "no qualities in trade that should entitle a man to superiority. It is quite true that we can suppose a merchant to be a man of an enlarged mind, such as Addison in the *Spectator* describes Sir Andrew Freeport to have been. We may suppose any fictitious character; we may suppose a philosophical day-labourer who is happy in reflecting that by his labour he contributes to the support of his fellow-creatures but we find no such philosophical day-labourers. A merchant may perhaps be a man of enlarged mind: but there is nothing in trade connected with an enlarged mind."

It is true that

> Who sweeps a room as for Thy laws
> Makes that and the action fine,

but the action is not fine in itself.

For mere wealth Johnson never had any respect. "Sir, the insolence of wealth will creep out," he said;

or, "Tradeswomen (I mean the wives of tradesmen) in the City who are worth from £10,000 to £15,000 are the worst creatures upon earth, grossly ignorant and thinking viciousness fashionable"; or, "There is indeed no employment however despicable from which a man may not promise himself more than competence when he sees thousands and myriads raised to dignity by no other merit than that of contributing to supply their neighbours with the means of sucking smoke through a tube of clay."

Indeed, much that was called business was, as he acutely saw, merely so called in order that the Puritan conscience might be allowed to indulge in it and yet boast itself free of the vice of gambling. Johnson characteristically preferred gambling under its own name to gambling under another.

> "Who is ruined by gaming?" he asked. "You will not find six instances in an age. There is a strange rout made about deep play; whereas you have many more people ruined by adventurous trade and yet we do not hear such an outcry against it."

When the voices of those who debate about efficiency and commercial organisation are at last still, it is Johnson who has said the one certainly true thing on the question: "Sir, trade could not be managed by those who manage it if it had much difficulty."

Another remark of Johnson's was the one that no man is really happy "but when he is drunk." It would be a mistake to take this with profound gravity, as it would be a mistake to take with profound gravity his ethical precept that one might toss snails over the garden wall, provided that one's neighbour was a Dissenter. Yet it would be equally a mistake to dismiss it as a mere flippancy. The point is that no one can be perfectly happy so long as he is conscious of time. For, however pleasant may be his state of mind at the moment, if he is conscious of time he is conscious that that state of mind will pass away when the external circumstances which created it have passed away. The only real refuge from time is of course in the pure pleasures of the reason. Yet even irrational pleasures can be enjoyed in the illusion that they are timeless. Great excitement will produce such an illusion, but drink produces it more satisfactorily. Driving in a post-chaise was one of Johnson's keenest pleasures. "Life has not many better things than this," he said of it. Yet, when Boswell asked if he would not bracket it with drunkenness as a producer of perfect happiness, he answered, "No, sir, you are driving rapidly from something or to something." Drunkenness alone was absolutely good.

He had no opinion of history. Once, when Charles James Fox insisted on talking to him of the Catilinarian conspiracy, he "withdrew his attention and thought about Tom Thumb." The study of history, he argued, was not a valuable study, for we "know nothing but a few facts and dates." "The colouring was conjectural," he added.

It is the opinion of Boswell that he made this remark primarily to annoy Gibbon, who happened to be present. Whether that was his motive or not, the remark raises a very interesting and debatable point. History, it has been said, is philosophy teaching by example, and the only trouble seems to be that, if you select your examples with a little skill, there is no limit to the philosophies which can use history to bolster themselves up.

Let us take the greatest of all historical questions, that of the Christian revelation and of the many things which have been done in the name of that revelation. Both its supporters and its opponents are apt to appeal to history. But surely such an appeal, from whichever side it come, is the appeal of a man who argues in a vicious circle. One can only judge concerning the past by applying to the evidence certain standards of right and wrong; by, as Johnson put it, "balancing probabilities" and balancing possibilities; that is to say, by applying to it a certain ethical and metaphysical system. The historical evidence for the Christian revelation is not, as Johnson admitted to Boswell in his argument upon Hume, strong enough to convince a man against his metaphysics. It is an obvious absurdity then first to use your metaphysics to interpret your history and then to turn round and boast that your history has proved your metaphysics.

History has a certain quasi-parabolic value. Do not use your history to establish your metaphysics. But you may very well, after having adopted for other reasons a metaphysical system, use history very aptly to illustrate that system.

I think that on the whole history did more harm in Johnson's day than it does in this. It had not then been found out. In the eighteenth century you might say, "History teaches us," and then pretend that all history was but an extended example of some pet little fad of your own. If only you wrote well enough you might even be believed. And the period of history to which Johnson particularly objected was that of republican Rome, to which it was then the fashion to appeal for fantastic examples of civic excellence. "I know not," he wrote, "why anyone but a schoolboy in his declamation should whine over the commonwealth of Rome."

The collapse of the too large hopes of the French Revolution and the ebbs and flows in the fashions of history have made us a little more sceptical than was the generation of Johnson, though not nearly sceptical enough. History can to-day teach us at least one great lesson. We learn from history that there is very little to be learnt from history. We learn from it also, if we are wise, a decent scepticism concerning political panaceas. There has never been a Golden Age—at least since the Fall. For, under any constitution, power must be put into the hands of men; and men abuse power.

All these things Johnson knew very well. He knew them so well that he did not need history to teach them to him. And his objection, I fancy, was not really so much to history as to historians. He knew that human nature did not change. He objected to the historian who told him that it did. "All history," it has been said, "is a history of one's own century." Johnson was doubtless ignorant of the accidents of the past: of its substance, of what its men were like, he had far too keen a sense to be willing to spend much time in learning what the present said about them. He was avid to study "modes of life." It was only that small part that "kings or lords can cause or cure" which he found tedious. He, more almost than any other person, was the type of the normal man. The normal man does not take kindly to history. His objection to it is that it does not mention him.

Somewhat similar was Johnson's attitude towards the French.

> "The French have large squares in their windows—they make good iron palisades. Their meals are gross,"

or:

> "At night we went to a comedy. I neither saw nor heard—Drunken women—Mrs. Th. preferred one to the other,"

were the generalisations of his diary upon Paris. Certainly he said, and greatly enjoyed saying, a lot of stupid and ignorant things about the French. "For anything I see, all foreigners are fools," he quoted with approbation from Meynell.

He was, as is often said and justly said, a great Englishman. Delany, in his letter to Swift, mentions, among his friend's qualities, that of "invincible patriotism to a country which he did not love." There was no such tragic twist of "faith unfaithful" about Johnson. He was a great Englishman, and a man who loved the things which he praised and praised the things which he loved. Yet fundamentally his quarrel with the French was a family quarrel. Because he was a citizen of the province of Europe he did not need to go to France to be taught how to live. "The Continent," he said of his day, with exaggeration but still with only too much truth, "is a part of the world divided between bigotry and atheism." To-day the boot is on the other foot. If we would learn that men should sit, that men should talk, that men should own property, that "Monarch Reason" should rule, it is coming to it that we must go to the Continent to learn these things. It was not necessary in eighteenth-century England where they could be learnt at the Mitre Tavern round the corner.

Johnson was careless of his Anglo-Saxon origins. "All our religion, almost all our law, almost all our arts, almost all that sets us above savages has come to us from the shores of the Mediterranean," he wrote, a generation before a Corsican lawyer's son renewed the world through the incomparable lucidity of the

Code Napoléon. "The great object of travelling," he added, "is to see the shores of the Mediterranean."

It is important not to be unfairly generous to Johnson. To take his jokes about foreigners seriously would be very silly. Yet at the same time it is only right to insist that, of all kinds of jokes, jokes about foreigners are the stupidest, the most tedious, the most dangerous. If a generation has arisen which really does take Johnson's nonsense seriously, Johnson must bear a little bit of the responsibility. Yet had he foreseen that his silliness about Frenchmen would be used as evidence of the cousinship of England with the drill-sergeants of Potsdam, he would, we may be sure, have dealt with the whole Nordic tale as he dealt with Boswell's ill-judged praise of the people of Otaheite. "Sir, do not cant in favour of savages."

For in an age in which the evil experiment of the Hohenzollern was for the first time becoming dangerous to Europe, when the pious, seeing that the Prussians were strong, were bidding us forgive them the trespasses that they had committed against Maria Theresa, when the Radical was hailing Frederick as *le roi philosophe* and the Tory rejoicing that another absolute monarch had risen to power, it was no wise cosmopolitan who dared to call a spade a spade, but blind old John Bull Johnson who first branded Prussianism as the evil and contemptible business that it was. He did not deny Frederick the Great's real services to Prussia, but he merely refused to be taken

REMARKABLE CHARACTERS WHO WERE AT TUNBRIDGE WELLS WITH RICHARDSON IN 1748, FROM A DRAWING IN HIS POSSESSION WITH REFERENCES IN HIS OWN WRITING

in by him. To Johnson a man, whether he were king or pickpocket, who took what was not his was a thief, and he who took it at the expense of other people's lives was also a coward. He dismissed Frederick in the perfect and stinging phrase of "Voltaire's lackey."

Poor Carlyle is so shocked that he hardly knows what to do. He can only lament the great man's blind spot. And when he finds that, in Paris, Johnson caught "no feeblest glimpse of those D'Alemberts and Diderots and of the strange, questionable work they did; solely some Benedictine priests to talk kitchen-Latin with," he can only lament again. Yet to-day neither encyclopædists nor Hohenzollerns stand quite so high as once they did, and there are many who are beginning to see that Johnson was a wiser man than Carlyle and a wiser man than all his generation; that perhaps he found more sense in the "kitchen-Latin" of the "Benedictine priests" than in the "strange, questionable work" of D'Alembert and Diderot; that perhaps he found Europe which almost all the rest of England was so soon to lose.

This is not rhetoric. Of the ideas of thinkers, some are interesting for themselves, others for their historical importance. So of eighteenth-century French thinkers, Voltaire or Montesquieu perhaps are of interest because of their ideas, the encyclopædists merely because of the effect of their ideas. What did D'Alembert or Diderot ever say that was especially memorable or intelligent? Carlyle, his mind full of the enormous effort of the Revolution, is rightly greedy for every detail about the lives of those who played their little part in bringing it about and is angry with Johnson because he does not satisfy this curiosity. Yet Johnson, visiting Paris before the Revolution and not foreseeing it, could not be expected to share this greed and should not be blamed because he sought out the company where he would find most entertainment. Benedictines were doubtless more intelligent than encyclopædists.

Nor would Johnson swallow the baits with which Imperial emigration authorities try to entrap the unwary—"the epidemical fury of emigration," as he called it in the *Journey to the Western Islands*. The European—at least, if his pleasures are at all intellectual—was not, Johnson claimed, happy out of Europe. "A man," he said, "had better have £10,000 at the end of ten years passed in England than £20,000 at the end of ten years passed in India." "A man of any intellectual enjoyment," he told Lord Monboddo, "will not easily go and immerse himself and his posterity for ages in barbarism."

In those things which pass ordinarily for amusements Johnson found small pleasure. He sided with Aristotle concerning the sea. In his opinion "a ship was worse than a gaol. There is in a gaol better air, better company, better conveniency of every kind; and a ship has the additional disadvantage of being in danger." As for a sailor's happiness, he confessed, "I cannot account for that any more than I can account for other strange perversions of imagination."

He held a similar opinion of hunting. "It is very strange and very melancholy that the paucity of human pleasures should persuade us ever to call hunting one of them." "Hunting" was "the labour of the savages of North America but the amusement of the gentlemen of England." It amused because "man feels his own vacuity less in action than when at rest."

Johnson once said that he counted a day lost upon which he did not make a new acquaintance. Many volumes—and, for those with patience to read them, many very interesting volumes—could be filled with accounts of his first meetings. A selection must suffice. I have already told the story of two of his first meetings—that with Boswell and that with Reynolds. Two more at any rate we must tell.

Johnson used sometimes to go and read in the library of "the Queen's House." One February afternoon, as the old man was seated in front of the fire there, engrossed in a book, he was suddenly interrupted by Dr. Barnard, the librarian.

"Sir, here is the King."

Johnson sprang to his feet.

George III has undoubtedly been unfairly blamed by his enemies. Yet even his friends cannot pretend that he was a very great man and even he would not have boasted of his literary interests. "Great part of Shakespeare" was "sad stuff, only one must not say so," and one may suspect that, if his most private opinion could have been discovered, "great part" of *Rasselas* or the *Rambler* was very little better. Yet he had, I suppose, been coached for this interview as kings are coached, and he acquitted himself surprisingly well.

Johnson was delighted. "Sir," he said to Barnard, "they may talk of the King as they will; but he is the finest gentleman that I have ever seen"; and when, a few nights afterwards at Sir Joshua Reynolds', they questioned him on the interview, Johnson began to philosophise.

"I find it does a man good to be talked to by his Sovereign. In the first place a man cannot be in a passion——"

"Here some question interrupted him," and what, in the second place or in the third place, were the advantages of being talked to by George III a curious posterity can never know.

All the time that Johnson was telling Reynolds' company of his experiences, Goldsmith, that odd mixture of greatness and pettiness, lay at full length on a sofa apart, ostentatiously sulking. He would have given his eyes to have had such an interview himself and he could not bear to hear of Johnson's distinction. Thus he lay for a time while Johnson thundered on. Suddenly the good in his curious soul won its victory. "He sprung from the sofa." He rushed across the room to Johnson, butted into the circle and shouted out in quaint congratulation:

"Well, you acquitted yourself in this conversation

better than I should have done; for I should have bowed and stammered through the whole of it."

So much for George III and the peculiar Goldsmith, who, though "he could talk with crowds nor lose the common touch," could never have "walked with kings and kept his virtue." Johnson's other meeting was with Wilkes.

It was the strange ambition of the amazing Boswell to bring together Samuel Johnson and John Wilkes. Their host was to be Mr. Dilly, the bookseller, at whose supper-table Boswell promised to produce Johnson one night when Wilkes was to be present.

He attacked Johnson, therefore, and gave him an invitation from Dilly.

"I will wait upon him," said Johnson.

"Provided, sir, I suppose," said Boswell, "that the company he is to have is agreeable to you."

Johnson rose as he was intended to rise.

"What do you mean, sir?" he cried. "What do you take me for? Do you think I am so ignorant of the world as to prescribe to a gentleman what company he is to have at his table?"

Boswell: I beg your pardon, sir, for wishing to prevent you from meeting people whom you might not like. Perhaps he may have some of what he calls his patriotic friends with him.

Johnson: Well, sir, and what then? What care I for his patriotic friends? Poh!

Boswell: I should not be surprised to find Jack Wilkes there.

Johnson: And if Jack Wilkes should be there, what is that to me, sir? My dear friend, let us have no more of this. I am sorry to be angry with you; but really it is treating me strangely to talk to me as if I could not meet any company whatever occasionally.

Boswell: Pray forgive me, sir. I meant well, but you shall meet whoever comes for me.

Boswell had thus won the first victory. But the meeting was still far from effected. When Wednesday came, he went round to Johnson's house and found, as he half feared, that Johnson had quite forgotten his engagement.

"How is this, sir?" cried Boswell in despair. "Don't you recollect that you are to dine at Mr. Dilly's?"

Johnson answered that he had forgotten, and that he had arranged to dine with Miss Williams.

Miss Williams had therefore to be pacified. It was nervous work, but at last she was got to say that Johnson might go.

"Frank, a clean shirt," Johnson bawled out, and soon afterwards he was on the way to Mr. Dilly's.

At dinner he was put next to Wilkes. At first Johnson was obviously uncomfortable in the company, but for shame did not dare to complain. Wilkes played up magnificently. His manners were perfect, and he was determined to make himself agreeable. He plied Johnson with food.

"Pray give me leave, sir; it is better here a little of the brown—some fat, sir—a little of the stuffing—some gravy—let me have the pleasure of giving you some butter. Allow me to recommend a squeeze of this orange; or the lemon perhaps may have more zest."

"Sir, sir, I am obliged to you, sir," Johnson could not but stammer out.

Gradually he thawed, and before long he and Wilkes had joined hands for a railing attack upon Boswell and the Scotch. The jeers Boswell good-humouredly bore. They but added to his triumph. Before the night was out Johnson and Wilkes had found themselves to have in common another and a more serious opinion—their detestation of George II.

Johnson, perhaps you may say, hated George II because he was not a king and Wilkes because he was. The Tory who believed that Parliament could not settle the succession, because kingship was a sacramental thing, joined hands with the Radical who doubted whether there ought to be any succession at all. Yet there was between the two something too deep to be merely shrugged away with the silly phrase that extremes meet. The extremes of Toryism and Radicalism have at least one thing in common, which neither Whig nor Liberal can ever come to; they share "God's scorn for all men governing," that great scorn which caused the Tory Goldsmith to write:

> Princes and lords may flourish and may fade;
> A breath can make them, as a breath hath made,

which drove the savage but towering genius of Dean Swift into madness at the thought that men had sometimes the insolence to be proud, and which was marked both by the "riot" of Wilkes and by the "rest" of Johnson.

So little does the Radical think of government that he will pull down the mighty from their seats. So little does the Tory think of government that he will not even bother to do that, for he knows that to do so would be but to make room for someone else and that someone else would be just as bad. "If every man that wears a laced coat (that he can pay for) was extirpated, who would miss them?" asked Johnson. The French Revolution was soon to put this very interesting speculation to the test.

The Radical and the Tory shared also a bias against common people being interfered with if it was not absolutely necessary. Seventy years before Sir Robert Peel reformed it, Johnson was protesting against the barbarities of our penal code and was returning again and again to the injustice and folly of the system of imprisonment for debt.

Wilkes too would have sympathised with Johnson's protest against the incarceration in a madhouse of his poor friend, Kit Smart. In that protest there was something of the spirit of Dickens, or of a spirit even nobler than that of Dickens.

> "I did not think he ought to be shut up. His infirmities were not noxious to society. He insisted

> on people praying with him and I had as lief pray with Kit Smart as anyone else.

And then he added characteristically, "Another charge was that he did not love clean linen and I have no passion for it." Wilkes would have sympathised with Johnson's protest against the abuse, though Johnson would have been too wise to sympathise with Wilkes's naïve faith that you would get rid of such abuses by merely altering the Constitution.

How vivid, even after one hundred and fifty years, is that scene at little Mr. Dilly's dinner-table! The year was 1776—the year, perhaps you may call it, of the beginning of the new world. What would those two strange, great men have thought if they could have foreseen what this new world was to be? Everything that Johnson loathed, everything that Wilkes loved, was to conquer—the freedom of the Press, freedom of love, decline of dogmatic religion—and the end of it all was not to be, as Johnson would have foretold, mere chaos, nor, as Wilkes would have hoped, a more splendid freedom.

Ours is both a richer and a kinder England than was that of Johnson and Wilkes, and these are important advantages. Yet I do not think that it is a freer England. The end of it all, of Wilkes's Radicalism and Johnson's Toryism, is that men bearing the name of Radicals are imposing on the poor a tyranny in some ways more merciless than any against which Wilkes ever protested, a tyranny which, had he lived to see it, would perhaps have made even Samuel Johnson bid them throw open the doors and roar out with a voice of thunder the great battle-cry of "Wilkes and Liberty."

Let us see exactly what was Johnson's quarrel with Wilkes. Wilkes, as the Gordon rioters were to discover, was no silly advocate of mobs for mobs' sake. He was a democrat. Now Johnson did not especially object to democracy. Democracy would, indeed, have seemed to him a silly form of government. "Pooh, leave me alone," he said to the crowd that bade him shout for "Wilkes and Liberty." "I at least am not ashamed to own that I care for neither the one nor the other."

Yet he agreed with La Fontaine that

> Le sage dit selon les temps,
> Vive le roi, vive la ligue.

Democracy with all its absurdities, as he would have thought them, was one of the forms of government which he would not have given half a guinea to change. "For forms of government let fools contest." What Johnson did demand was that morals should be recognised as objective and absolute. That exemption from morals which he had refused to King Frederick he refused equally to King Demos. He objected, not to democracy, but to Democratism, to adopt the phraseology of M. Maritain—that is, to the notion that the General Will is divine, that majorities have the right to make up morals and that wrong becomes right simply because it happens to have been voted.

The point of Johnson's objection was not such a one, perhaps, as Wilkes would very readily have grasped. Yet Johnson saw clearly enough that Wilkism would lead, not only to democracy, but to Democratism. Medmenham Abbey would not be content with the mild Liberalism of the Reform Club.

It is important not to seem that very vulgar thing, "a declaimer against the times," nor to appear the sort of man who catches the 10.15 in order to attend a meeting of protest against the invention of machinery. It is as important not to shrink from the conclusions of Reason through a silly and cowardly fear of being called reactionary. Even if we are behind the times, there are some times which it is a very good thing to be behind. Let us put the case with as little rhetoric as possible and be held responsible only for what we say. The argument, it will be recognised, is Signor Ferrero's.

Rousseau preached that the General Will was infallible; the utilitarians that demand should create supply. That is to say, both in morals and economics people were to have a right to a thing simply because they wanted it. The economic was a necessary consequence of the political doctrine. These men carried a step farther the evil subjectivism of Hamlet:

> There's nothing either good or bad,
> But wanting makes it so.

They derive logically from Wilkes's Radicalism.

The world then was invited to want as much as it possibly could, and on this invitation our industrial system was built. Until 1914 that invitation did not bring us to disaster for two reasons—first, because the exploitation of new field after new field of raw material made it still possible to keep pace with the demands of human greed; second, because only a part of the world had as yet learnt to accept the invitation. Nations and even continents were still willing to be exploited.

To-day the time is in sight when there will be no more virgin territories to divide among the clamorous. The time is also in sight when the rest of the world, having learnt from Europe to be greedy and to use machines, will refuse any longer to allow the products of the whole world to be enjoyed all but exclusively by a small fraction of the world's inhabitants. When the whole world demands a higher standard of living, how is that demand going to be met?

You murmur that science will progress? There will be new inventions? But, however rapid the advance of science, it can never advance as rapidly as human greed. "It is not given to man to foresee the future," and all prophecies may be false. Yet few seem safer than the prophecy that the twentieth century will be a century of gigantic economic scrambles leading to terrible conflict, the end of which no man can tell. If that be so, we shall be unjust if we turn in too great anger on those men who, revolting against very real abuses, preached to us the doctrines of which these conflicts are the unforeseen conclusion. We shall be as unjust if we do not turn in gratitude to those greater men who, as conscious of the abuses, yet foresaw what would be the conclusion of the doctrines; who did not foresee, indeed, how or when the world would come to its disaster but who yet held so certainly by the central traditions of our race that they condemned when they were merely crimes all those injustices which we to-day are beginning to condemn when we have discovered that they were also blunders. "Depend upon it, this rage of trade will destroy itself. You and I shall not see it; but the time will come when there will be an end of it!"

Before the dinner was finished the company "had an accession of Mrs. Knowles, the Quaker lady," and, as Wilkes "waggishly insisted," "Johnson showed fervent signs of the corresponding charms of the fair Quaker." It was this Mrs. Knowles who at another meeting won from Johnson very enthusiastic praise. An argument had arisen whether or not God could show favour in the bestowal of His love. Johnson maintained that He could not.

"But, doctor," said Mrs. Knowles, "our Saviour had twelve apostles, yet there was one whom He loved. John was called 'the disciple whom Jesus loved.' "

Loose language speaks of Johnson as prejudiced. A prejudiced person is one who has pre-judged, who has formed his conclusion before he has heard the arguments, and who will not afterwards listen to the arguments. If that be so, no man who ever lived was less prejudiced than Johnson on any matter about which he really cared. He was rather like a starving man hungry for bread in his eagerness to hear any new argument. Dr. Adams, growing weary, thought that surely we had by now sufficient evidence of the immortality of the soul. "I wish for more," cried Johnson, with all the appetite of Oliver Twist.

This appetite Mrs. Knowles had satisfied. She had thrown for him new light upon the nature of God. He capitulated at once.

"Very well indeed, madam. You have said very well," he cried.

Boswell was by, note-book out, we may be sure, and ready to improve the shining hour.

"A fine application. Pray, sir, had you ever thought of it?" he asked.

"I had not, sir," said the happy Johnson, with enormous emphasis.

CHAPTER VII

JOHNSON AND THE SERAGLIO

Such is a small selection from the table-talk of Dr. Johnson. It is by his table-talk, when all is said and done, that he is best known to us, and it is likely enough that but for it he would be hardly known to us to-day at all. That is a very small point. No wise man can care very much whether he "belongs to the ages" or not. They are silly things to belong to. So, even though it may be his table-talk which causes anyone in the twentieth century to think of writing a character-sketch of Samuel Johnson, yet it would be a very poor character-sketch which left the impression that his table-talk was all that there was of him.

There is another side of Johnson than that which the American tourist tries somewhat pathetically to recapture at the Cheshire Cheese. Ruskin said that if there were no walls to conceal from us the misery of the poor we should never be able to sit down to a hearty meal. To Johnson such talk was nauseating. The notion that no man should begin to take any pleasure until the world was first made perfect would have seemed to him ridiculous. And we may be sure that, had he been alive to hear the remark, he would have replied to it, "Then, sir, let us thank God for walls."

Nevertheless, he did not at all possess the talent for keeping the poor out of sight of the rich. Mrs. Thrale, who by the time that she came to write about him was by no means a wholly favourable witness, records that he loved the poor as she had never seen anyone else love them. Nor did he ever pretend to the affectation of being indifferent to others' love for him. Approbation, he confessed, was "valuable if from the meanest of human beings."

When Johnson was at home, beggars "waited his coming out," and he records it as a happiness that they did so. Of Swift he wrote, whether justly or not, "His beneficence was not graced with tenderness or civility; he relieved without pity and assisted without kindness so that those who were fed by him could hardly love him." Such a fault was never Johnson's. As he went home at night he would put pennies into the hands of the sleeping street urchins that they might be able to afford a breakfast the next morning.

Records of his quaintly humorous acts of charity you can find in his *Prayers and Meditations,* the more revealing because they were only published after his death and were never intended for a public eye. On Easter Day of 1764 he records that he, "seeing a poor girl at the sacrament, gave her a crown though Hart's Hymns in her hands," and an even stranger little story began on the same day, when "I saw at the sacrament a man meanly dressed whom I have always seen there at Easter." On Easter Day of the next year:

> "I invited home with me the man whose pious behaviour I had for several years observed on this day and found him a kind of Methodist, full of texts but ill-instructed. I talked to him with temper and offered him twice wine which he refused. I suffered him to go without the dinner which I had purposed to give him. I thought this day that there was something irregular and particular in his look and gesture; but having intended to invite him to acquaintance and having a fit opportunity by finding him near my own seat after I had missed him I did what I had at first designed and am sorry to have been so much disappointed. Let me not be prejudiced hereafter against the appearance of piety in mean persons who, with indeterminate notions and perverse or inelegant conversation, perhaps are doing all they can."

Johnson had at one time and another, according to a very frank page of Boswell, made use of prostitutes for his own pleasure. Whatever may be the legitimate empire of prudery, it is certain that it is as little possible to write the life of Johnson without mentioning that page as it would be to write the life of St. Mary Magdalene without mentioning a similar page. Johnson was no ratiocinating sermoniser, inhuman, hardly feeling temptations of such a kind or, if he felt them, conquering them easily. It was remorse which led him to love and which caused him to behave towards prostitutes with a quite amazing tenderness. To the old and the destitute of every sort he was unstinted in his charity. The best of all panegyrics upon him is perhaps the measured and gentlemanly censure of Sir John Hawkins. "He had a natural imbecility about him, arising from humanity and pity to the sufferings of his fellow-creatures, that was prejudicial to his interests."

When people objected that the money which he gave to the poor was only spent upon gin and tobacco he answered that it was savage to deny them those few, coarse pleasures which the rich disdained, and he who was sometimes loud of voice at the tables of gentlemen never forgot that "a severe and punctilious temper is ill-qualified for transactions with the poor." They asked him once why he always gave to beggars.

"Madam," he said, "to enable them to beg on."

"There was that woman to whom you yesterday gave half a crown. Why, she was at church to-day in long sleeves and ribands."

"Well, my dear, and if it gave the woman pleasure, why should she not wear them?"

If you would have an example of his charitable kindness, read the story of his parting from his mother's old servant, Catharine Chambers.

"Sunday, Oct. 18, 1767. Yesterday, Oct. 17, at about ten in the morning, I took my leave for ever of my old friend, Catharine Chambers, who came to live with my mother about 1724 and has been but little parted from us since. She buried my father, my brother and my mother. She is now fifty-eight years old.

"I desired all to withdraw, then told her that we were to part for ever, that as Christians we should part with prayer; and that I would if she was willing say a short prayer beside her. She expressed great desire to hear me: and held up her poor hands as she lay in bed with great fervour while I prayed, kneeling by her, nearly in the following words:

" 'Almighty and most merciful Father, Whose loving kindness is over all Thy works, behold, visit and relieve this Thy servant who is grieved with sickness. Grant that the sense of her weakness may add strength to her faith and seriousness to her repentance. And grant that by the help of Thy Holy Spirit after the pains and labours of this short life we may all obtain everlasting happiness through Jesus Christ, our Lord, for Whose sake hear our prayers. Amen. Our Father, etc.'

"I then kissed her. She told me that to part was the greatest pain she had ever felt and that she hoped we should meet again in a better place. I expressed with swelled eyes and great emotion of tenderness the same hopes. We kissed and parted. I humbly hope to meet again and part no more."

Nor was his charity to dependants confined to the death-bed, foolish and cheap as it would be to sneer at it even if it had been. Of his strange, ill-assorted household everybody has read, and, though there can be no sense at all in being blind to the mere comedy of that household, it would be very shallow to see in it nothing more than the comic.

Of his pension of £300 he only professed to allow himself £100 a year. The other £200 were to be spent on charity, and it was the opinion of the Thrales that he never did, in fact, spend upon himself more than £70 or £80. The rest all went to the upkeep of his "seraglio," as he called it in a phrase which was to be afterwards quoted in order to clear the name of a great English statesman.

Of the seraglio the first member was Miss Williams. Miss Williams had been a friend of his wife. She had come to stay with them in order to undergo an operation for cataract. The operation had been a failure and she had remained on in the house until very many years after Mrs. Johnson's death. She was blind and peevish, and, as we read of her, it is hard to find anything likeable in her character. She seems to have been quite unconscious of Johnson's kindness to her. She was of gentle birth but, as far as can be discovered and in spite of Johnson's generous praise, of little intellect. Johnson would often sacrifice his main pleasure—that of conversation with his friends—in order to stay at home and spend the evening with her, small though he knew the chance to be that she would say anything that would at all interest such a mind as his. His reward was that she was continually nagging at him for not staying at home more frequently. The only service, as far as can be discovered, which she rendered him was to sit up at nights and make his tea when he came in. That this was a considerable service, when one considers the irregularity and eccentricity of Johnson's hours, need not be at all denied. Yet it was but little to give in return for his friendship, to say nothing of his charity, for but for him she would have been hard put to it to find a roof to put over her head or a maid to serve her. As Johnson confessed to Boswell, "Age and sickness and pride have made her so peevish that I was forced to bribe the maid to stay with her by a secret stipulation of half a crown over her wages." Nevertheless the little service that Johnson asked of Miss Williams she gave grudgingly. Yet at her death he said that she had been to him as a sister.

Miss Williams had a little money of her own—about £40 a year, it appears. She was the only one of the household who seems to have made any contribution, however small, to its expenses. Its second member was Robert Levett. Levett had been a waiter at a doctor's coffee-house in Paris. He had succeeded in picking up from his patrons a smattering of medicine and had then set up, without of course any kind of qualification, as a poor man's doctor, being paid by his patients in whatever commodity might be available, but usually in gin. He was, as Johnson declared, the only man who ever got drunk from motives of prudence, since, if he did not take the gin which was offered, he would get nothing at all. A kind of self-respect prevented him from gratuitous attendance. "He would swallow what he did not like, nay, what he knew would injure him, rather than go home with an idea that his skill had been without recompense."

Johnson's acquaintance with him began, it seems, in 1746, but how it began Boswell does not seem to have known, nor, so far as I am aware, has anybody since been able to discover. "He was of a strange, grotesque appearance, stiff and formal in his manner and seldom said a word while any company was present," writes Boswell.

In 1762 he married a prostitute who, although at the time only able to offer the very mildly attractive hospitality of "a coal hole in Fetter Lane," had yet represented to him and persuaded him that she had rich relations. Needless to say, her tale was wholly false, and soon afterwards the couple were separated from one another and Levett returned to Johnson. As Goldsmith said to Boswell, "Levett now becomes miserable and that ensures the protection of Johnson." He continued to reside in Johnson's house until his death in 1782.

On his death Johnson wrote one of his best known pieces of verse:

> Well tried through many a varying year,
> See Levett to the grave descend,
> Officious, innocent, sincere,
> Of every friendless name the friend.
>
> In misery's darkest cavern known,
> His ready help was ever nigh;
> Where hopeless anguish pour'd his groan,
> And lonely want retired to die.
>
> No summons mocked by dull delay,
> No petty gains disdain'd by pride;
> The modest wants of every day
> The toil of every day supplied.
>
> His virtues walked their narrow round,
> Nor made a pause, nor found a void;
> And sure the eternal Master found
> His single talent well employed.

This is not perhaps great poetry, any more than anything else that Johnson ever wrote was great poetry, but it has a special and a very noble place in literature. It is one of the very few entirely sincere tributes paid by one whom the world calls a success to one whom the world calls a failure. Of this there is, naturally, no consciousness. Had there been consciousness of it, it probably would not have been sincere. It is in the complete sincerity of the verses that their attractiveness lies. It had obviously never for a moment occurred to Johnson to despise a man because he had but "a single talent" and was content to employ it. Burke said of Boswell that he had so much natural amiability that amiability was in him hardly a virtue. In the same way it might be said that snobbery was by nature so completely absent from Johnson's character that lack of snobbery was hardly a virtue in him. He must be one of the very few who never in their lives even felt the temptation to sneer at anyone for being poor.

It appears that Johnson greatly overestimated Levett's medical skill. His science was, in truth, extremely crude. Yet Johnson insisted upon being attended by him and even said that, were the whole College of Surgeons to be present, he would not be satisfied until he had taken Levett's opinion.

Next to Levett comes Mrs. Desmoulins. She was the daughter of Dr. Swinfen, a Lichfield physician and Johnson's godfather. Johnson had had a quarrel with the father because he had revealed secrets which Johnson had confided to him in his professional capacity. But, when he died in poverty, Johnson nevertheless provided a home for the daughter and for the daughter's child as well. He made them an allowance of a twelfth of his pension.

Then there was Frank, the negro servant—a legacy, as has been already said, from his friend, Dr. Bathurst. What services Frank performed for Johnson has never, I believe, been discovered. He did not cook for him nor did he wait upon him. As, if Sir Walter Raleigh's interpretation of a curious note of Johnson's in his commentary on *King John* is correct, he never discovered that people had different boots for their different feet, and as at any rate the condition of his person and his clothes was always such that they could not have been made more disreputable even by an artist of neglect, it would be an insult to any servant to suggest that he valeted for him. Likely enough, Frank would have been willing to do more if only Johnson had allowed him. He was ready enough to run messages whenever there were any to be run. Yet it does not seem likely that all his services to Johnson amounted to very much. What services in return for this little Johnson performed for Frank it is much easier to learn. He put him to school; he wrote to him continually; he cared for him in every way. And even the humble Frank had his little influence on history.

It was, I make no doubt, his affection for his negro servant which was the first cause of Johnson's vigorous opposition to, and detestation of, slavery. From his general principles one would not have been surprised to have found him arguing in favour of some system of enlightened slavery as being "in accordance with the grand principle of subordination." Yet he did denounce it in language as violent and as ignorant as ever came out of Clapham. He opposed the white man in America with all the rancour with which Burke opposed the white man in India. The exploitation, whether of black man or of red, the whole substitution of Imperialism for morals, had never a more unflinching foe than Samuel Johnson.

His enmity carried him both into nobleness and into folly. He gave to "some very grave men" at Oxford the toast of "The next negro-insurrection in Jamaica," and even faithful Boswell was forced to make it clear in his Life that he was unable to follow his master in his opinions on this question.

It was this hatred of slavery which, with other things, was the reason of Johnson's very violent opposition to the American cause when that quarrel arose. He spoke of the "planters of America" as "a race of mortals whom, I suppose, no other man wishes to resemble," and told Mrs. Knowles, "I am willing to love all mankind except an American." He denounced them as hypocrites in demanding freedom for themselves while they maintained a system of slavery for the negroes.

Doubtless his principles would in any case have led him to take the royal side in this quarrel—and for reasons very much better than those which he gave. For, as he would have known had he been better informed, slavery was not a fortunate question to choose for the support of George III and opposition to the Americans, since one of the American complaints was that bills of the colonial assemblies for the abolition of the slave-trade had been continually vetoed by the Crown.

There remain but two members of the seraglio. One of them, a Miss Carmichael, was a shadowy figure. She survives in history only through the accident that Boswell, arriving from Scotland in 1778, found that Johnson, as an act of charity, had put her to sleep in his friend's bed. It is a minor immortality.

Last is the cat Hodge—Hodge, whom Boswell, who hated cats with an almost morbid hatred, could not abide; Hodge, for whom Johnson, unwilling that the servants should be degraded by being made to wait upon an animal, used himself to buy oysters at the oyster-bar; Hodge, whom Johnson loved but upon whom he has left us the unkind judgment that "I have had cats whom I liked better than this."

Such was the seraglio. It was not a happy family. "Williams," Johnson once wrote to Mrs. Thrale, "hates everybody; Levett hates Desmoulins and does not love Williams; Desmoulins hates them both; Poll"—that is, Miss Carmichael—"loves none of them." Nor did any of his dependants, save perhaps the negro Frank, seem ever to have shown Johnson the smallest gratitude for all that he did for them. Nor—what is more extraordinary—does Johnson seem in the least to have expected any gratitude.

CHAPTER VIII

JOHNSON AND DEATH

The charity and long-suffering even of Samuel Johnson were not inexhaustible, and it had been his custom, when things were no longer to be borne, to seek refuge with the Thrales at Streatham. In 1781 Thrale had died of over-eating and in 1782, as has been already recorded, Streatham ceased any longer to be a second home to him. The last two years of a life, the whole of which he himself described as "radically wretched," were certainly a very sad affair.

Johnson never made any pretence of concealing his fear of death. Rather would he continually harp on that fear with what some have thought to be an almost morbid iteration. Nor was his fear the least a fear of pain, whether the pain of the death-agony or of disease. There never, I suppose, lived a man more fearless of pain. His fear was entirely of the judgment.

It is sometimes, in the modern fashion, thought to be very ridiculous that a man should be afraid of hell. Yet, even if the Christian revelation be supposed false, reason would seem to teach us that, if there is a God, then either *"as flies are we to the gods; they plague us for their sport,"* or else He must necessarily, as Plato argued, reward virtue with happiness and punish vice with unhappiness. Virtue and happiness are certainly very ill equated in this world. It follows, then, that there will be a judgment passed upon us in a future state and rewards and punishments consequent upon the verdict of that judgment. As Johnson wrote in the *Adventurer*:

> "Since the common events of the present life happen alike to the good and bad, it follows from the justice of the Supreme Being that there must be another state of existence in which a just retribution shall be made and every man shall be happy and miserable according to his works."

He then is very foolish who does not live in continual and daily fear of hell. For neither Omnipotence nor Perfect Love, when once It has given to man the dangerous privilege of freedom, can prevent him from using that privilege in order to condemn his own soul if he chooses to do so; and it is presumption if a man says that he is certain in what state of mind he shall die. Johnson was surely right when he wrote:

> "I should not think the better of a man who should tell me on his death-bed he was sure of salvation. A man cannot be sure himself that he has divine intimation of acceptance."

Wiser than silly confidence is the great spirit of Goldsmith, who, when they asked him in his last moments, "Is your mind at ease?" answered, as such a man must have answered, "No, it is not."

> Christe, de tutam trepido quietem,
> Christe, spem præsta stabilem timenti:
> Da fidem certam, precibusque fidis
> Annue, Christe,

Johnson prayed.

It might on the other hand be thought that, if any soul could have faced with confidence that last judgment, it would have been the great, loving, lovable, charitable, truth-telling soul of Samuel Johnson, and that, like Veuillot, a man who, even as he, had given "confidence to truth" in a day of truth's desperate need, Johnson would have greeted the unseen, if not with a cheer, at the least with glad certainty.

> Dans ma lutte laborieuse
> La foi soutint mon cœur charmé;
> Ce fut donc une vie heureuse,
> Puisqu'enfin j'ai toujours aimé.
>
> Je fus pêcheur; et sur ma route,
> Hélas! j'ai chancelé souvent:
> Mais, grace à Dieu, vainqeur du doute,
> Je suis mort ferme et pénitent.
>
> J'espère en Jésus. Sur la terre
> Je n'ai pas rougi de Sa loi.
> Au dernier jour devant Son Père
> Il ne rougira pas de moi.

There are some Christians who, while still maintaining the faith of Christ, maintain it only with a sort of apology. Very happy are such men as Veuillot and Johnson, who, though born into an age when all the world was going wrong, yet never thought it necessary to apologise for being right and could boast at the end that one legitimate and most splendid of all boasts:

Je n'ai pas rougi de Sa loi.

They had never been ashamed of the freedom that God had given them.

Yet nothing could be more foolish than the trite saying that one of the rewards of virtue is an easy conscience. Whatever be the rewards of virtue, this is not one of them. The murderer or the bigamist is as likely to have an easy conscience as the saint or the martyr at the stake, for one of the simplest ways of setting your conscience at rest is to kill it. The genial, pleasant people who rub pleasantly along, neither greatly vicious nor greatly unselfish, doing the things that happen to come their way and not doing the things that do not come their way—all these have easy consciences. Their easy conscience is their reward. Not of such was Samuel Johnson. "The better a man is," said Johnson, "the more afraid is he of death, having a clearer view of infinite purity."

All the great and humble work which he had done for the love of God seemed only to have taught him how much more there was to be done. "When I survey my past life," he wrote in his *Prayers and Meditations*, "I discover nothing but a barren waste of time, with some disorders of body and disturbances of the mind which I hope that He That made me will suffer to extenuate many faults and excuse many deficiencies."

He one day confessed his fear of death at the table of his friend, Dr. Adams, the Master of Pembroke.

"As I cannot be sure that I have fulfilled the conditions on which salvation is granted," he said, "I am afraid I may be one of those who shall be damned."

"What do you mean by 'damned'?" asked Dr. Adams.

"Sent to hell, sir, and punished everlastingly," answered Johnson—as Boswell says, passionately and loudly.

They tried him with comforts of a metaphysical kind. If God was infinitely good, was it possible that He would condemn a human soul?

Johnson answered that God was infinitely good upon the whole but that, for the good of the whole, individuals had to suffer; therefore He was not infinitely good to every individual.

They then tried upon him comforts of a more directly theological kind.

"You seem, sir," said Mrs. Adams, "to forget the merits of our Redeemer."

"Madam," he answered, "I do not forget the merits of my Redeemer, but my Redeemer has said that He will set some on His right and some on His left."

Then he broke off.

"I'll have no more on't," he cried.

In the May of 1784 this conversation took place. By the end of that year he was dead. He met his death with all the courage and resignation of a brave man and seems at the end to have been granted more confidence than he had felt during his life.

Boswell was not there when it came to the last. Mrs. Thrale of course was not there. Of his younger friends, many—Garrick, Goldsmith, Beauclerk—were already dead. Windham and Langton, Burke and Reynolds, were those who were most frequently by his side.

> Te teneam moriens deficiente manu,

he murmured as he bade his last farewell to Langton, to whom he was perhaps more devoted than to any of the others. Burke was in tears. "My dear sir, you have always been too good to me," he sobbed out. Of Reynolds he begged three things—that he would forgive him a debt of £30; that he would read the Bible; that he would never paint on a Sunday. He sent money to pay off a debt of thirty years' standing to the son of Faden, the geographer, and of twenty years' standing to Hamilton, the printer.

Yet the last moment came, as it happened, when none but Frank Barber and Mrs. Desmoulins were with him. "His difficulty of breathing increased until about seven o'clock in the evening when Mr. Barber and Mrs. Desmoulins, who were sitting in the room, observing that the noise he made in breathing had ceased, went to the bed and found he was dead."

Thus died the great lover of all humble men and women. Gentlemen and philosophers and artists had gone their way and it was perhaps fitting that at the last only a crochety old lady and a poor nigger should have been there to look upon the face. The obituary column of the *Gentleman's Magazine* records: "On December 13 a little before seven in the evening, without a pang though long before oppressed with a complication of dreadful maladies, the great and good Dr. Samuel Johnson, the pride of English literature and of human nature."

His bones were laid in the only place fitted to receive the bones of one of the noblest of all Englishmen—in Westminster Abbey, near to the monument of his friend Oliver Goldsmith; and thus was the laughing prophecy fulfilled,

Forsitan et nostrum nomen miscebitur istis.

The story of Johnson's fear of hell does not make comfortable reading. "I know not," he said of his friend, "who will go to heaven if Langton does not." And we can but ask, if so great a soul as Samuel Johnson shall be lost, which of us can hope to be saved. Johnson seems, as I have said, to have imagined that at the last he received some intimation of acceptance. How much weight should be given to such things it is impossible to say. Perhaps his fears in this life were the punishment with which God afflicted him for those things in which he fell short of "perfect charity"—the charity which alone "casteth out fear." Perhaps with death all fear vanished away, and the angel said to his soul, as he said to that of Gerontius:

> It is because
> Then thou didst fear that now thou dost not fear,
> Thou hast forestalled the agony, and so
> For thee the bitterness of death is past.

INDEX

INDEX

INDEX

INDEX

INDEX

INDEX

INDEX

INDEX